D1523524

A Short History
of Taiwan

A SHORT HISTORY
OF TAIWAN

The Case for Independence

Gary Marvin Davison

Westport, Connecticut
London

Library of Congress Cataloging-in-Publication Data

Davison, Gary Marvin, 1951–
    A short history of Taiwan : the case for independence / Gary Marvin Davison.
        p. cm.
    Includes bibliographical references and index.
    ISBN 0–275–98131–2 (alk. paper)
    1.Taiwan—history. I. Title.
DS799.5.D38 2003
951.24′9—dc21   2003046961

British Library Cataloguing in Publication Data is available.

Library of Congress Catalog Card Number: 2003046961
ISBN: 0–275–98131–2

First published in 2003

Praeger Publishers, 88 Post Road West, Westport, CT 06881
An imprint of Greenwood Publishing Group, Inc.
www.praeger.com

Printed in the United States of America

The paper used in this book complies with the
Permanent Paper Standard issued by the National
Information Standards Organization (Z39.48–1984).

10 9 8 7 6 5 4 3 2 1

Copyright Acknowledgments

The author and publisher gratefully acknowledge permission for use of the following
materials:

Excerpts reprinted from Li P'eng, "The Rise of the Well-Versed Society: The Poetry
Renaissance in Comtemporary Taiwan," trans. Vincent Chang, *Sinorama,* December
1995, p. 129.

To Barbara Reed, my best friend and life companion,
whose love and confidence animate all my days

CONTENTS

ACKNOWLEDGMENTS

Many people have provided me with the inspiration, encouragement, and knowledge necessary to write this book. The people mentioned on these pages are those most firmly etched in my memory or most intimately involved in the production of this volume.

Several professors have served as important models of the teacher-scholar, given me the benefits of their extensive knowledge, and encouraged me to pursue further academic efforts. Such people include Bradley Carter and Ronald Davis at Southern Methodist University, Stephen Vlastos at the University of Iowa, and Edward L. Farmer and Vernon Ruttan at the University of Minnesota. My deep gratitude goes to all of these people for the confidence that they have shown in me at critical professional junctures.

The people of Taiwan have constantly amazed me, ever since I first stepped onto the island in 1980, with their drive to succeed economically and to persist in the development of a genuinely democratic polity. The ability of the Taiwanese people to endure over three centuries of outsider control while laying the foundation for a discreet nation-state drives the story told in this book and forms its central thesis. My thanks to all of those Taiwanese people who have so generously provided sources for my observations, interviews, and collection of documents.

Special thanks go to a number of people who have been good neighbors, friends, or fellow scholars during my periods of residence in Taiwan during 1980–81 and 1988–90, or trips back to the island in the summers of 1995, 1998, and 2003. Ouyang Qin offered a rental home in Tainan City and instructive comments on his experiences under the Japanese. In the Liushuang section of Shezi Village, located in Guantian Township of Tainan County, the family of patriarch Huang Kunshan has provided me with friendship and counsel ever since we met during my 1989–1990 period of fieldwork. Mr. Huang and his wife, Gao Zhupan, and their sons Huang Tiande, Huang Congming, and Huang Minggui have been constant sources of information on the agricultural and social life of rural Taiwan. The eminent scholars Wu Ts'ung-hsien, Huang Chun-chieh, and Hsiao Hsin-huang (Michael Hsiao) have generously put information in my head through various means: conversations, interviews, and materials from their voluminous scholarly writing.

   This book would never have come to the attention of the reading public without the confidence expressed in this volume by my agent, James Schiavone, and Praeger/Greenwood editor Heather Ruland Staines. My great thanks goes to them for their efforts in moving this book toward publication. The skilled team at Impressions Book and Journal Services deserves much commendation for their high quality editorial efforts at the book's production stage.

   As is the case with the remarkable people of Taiwan, family is the bedrock of all my endeavors. My enduring gratitude goes to my parents, Marvin and Betty Davison, for providing the early guidance that continues to serve as the foundation for my life. My great thanks also go to my wife's parents, Myron and Frances Reed, for the high level of interest and confidence that they have always expressed in my undertakings. To Barbara Reed, my best friend and life companion, and to Ryan Davison-Reed, my beloved son and generator of great questions, goes my deepest gratitude for their love and for their own sustained interest in the remarkable national polity of Taiwan.

INTRODUCTION

From autumn 1999 until March 2000, Chinese-language newspapers on Taiwan and mainland China, as well as English-language journals such as *Far Eastern Economic Review* specializing in news from East Asia, devoted a great deal of column space to the presidential campaign on Taiwan. Much of the concern on the part of the government of the People's Republic of China, the communist regime established on the mainland in 1949, lay in the candidacy of Chen Shuibian, the nominee of the Democratic Progressive Party. Though Chen was quickly moderating his views, both he and his party had a track record of advocating the position that Taiwan is an independent nation and should declare itself a separate political entity. This position is anathema to the government of the People's Republic, which maintains that Taiwan is historically linked to the mainland and rightfully belongs to the government that has power in the vast country of China.

History contains much to offer those who hold a view opposite to that espoused by the mainland regime. Taiwan was first incorporated into a Chinese empire in the late seventeenth century. The imperial government of the Qing dynasty (1644–1912) engaged in a hot debate as to whether to take administrative responsibility for the island, which had recently been ruled by a Ming dynasty (1368–1644) loyalist, who in turn had ousted a Dutch colonial regime. The court debate was eventually won by those arguing for incorporation of the island into the Chinese empire. Until the late nineteenth century, the Qing government ruled Taiwan with a great deal of help from local notables, who exercised authority in the country-side and in the local communities of a very contentious and frequently rebellious society on the southern fringe of the territories claimed by the Qing. The Qing court did elevate Taiwan to the status of province in 1887 and make substantial investments in the island society that took on new strategic value under the pressure of imperialists pressing in from Europe and Japan. But in 1895 Taiwan came under the control of the latter country as a spoil of war. Japan ruled Taiwan as a colony from 1895 until 1945.

Buoyed by support expressed by World War II's Allied forces in the Cairo Conference of 1943, the government of Chiang Kai-shek laid claim to Taiwan after the defeat of the Japanese in the Asia-Pacific theater. Chiang was the leader of the Guomindang, the party that at that time was engaged in a struggle with Mao Zedong's communists for control of the mainland. When Mao's soldiers emerged victorious in 1949, Chiang and his support-ers completed a retreat to Taiwan. Chiang maintained that his government still represented the Republic of China, established on the mainland with the fall of the Qing in 1912, and that one day he and his supporters would return to the mainland, defeat Mao and the communists, overturn the Peo-ple's Republic of China, and reinstate what the Guomindang saw as the rightful government, bearing the heritage and the name of the Republic of China. This sequence of events never materialized; after Chiang died in 1975, the government on Taiwan increasingly distanced itself from the vow of returning to the mainland through military engagement.

During the 1980s and 1990s Taiwan underwent a political miracle to match its famed economic miracle of the 1960s and 1970s. Martial law ended in 1987, and the Democratic Progressive Party and other opposition parties were legalized. The Guomindang leader, Lee Teng-hui, won the first popular election for president of the polity still bearing the Republic of China name in 1996. But in March 2000 the people of Taiwan went to the polls and did what the government of the mainland had feared and, through various threatening statements, had tried to prevent: They elected Chen Shuibian. A newly pragmatic Chen Shuibian vowed that he would not declare Taiwan's independence unless the mainland followed through on its most provocative threat, a military invasion of Taiwan. But in elect-ing Chen, the Taiwanese populace had shown that it was willing to opt for leaders with a pro-independence past, that it would not be intimidated by the Chinese mainland regime, and that the future of Taiwan would be a matter for the Taiwanese people to decide.

The political fate of Taiwan should indeed be a matter for the Taiwanese people to decide. The Taiwanese people may ultimately agree to some formula for unification with a mainland government. But Taiwanese society has not been under the political control of any regime simultaneously exercising power over all of mainland China since 1895. There exists in the unique history of the island, and its particular circumstances during the remarkable twentieth century, a compelling case for independence. In this book I endeavor to provide a concise and informative overview of the history of Taiwan and to make the case for independence. What happens to Taiwan as a political entity in the twenty-first century should be a matter for the Taiwanese people to decide. Should they choose independence and a new name such as the Republic of Taiwan, there is much in the Taiwanese past to justify such a choice.

NOTE ON ROMANIZATION

Pinyin is the romanization system used for most terms in this book. On Taiwan, the older Wade-Giles system still dominates the rendering of Chinese terms in romanized form. But other systems, including pinyin, are used on the island, and sometimes terms are rendered in a confusing combination of different systems. I use pinyin in this book because, for the most part, it more readily gives English speakers some feel for the sounds of Chinese words. An exception to the use of pinyin is found in my rendering of the longtime Guomindang leader's name as Chiang Kai-shek, the conventional usage that follows neither the pinyin nor the Wade-Giles system. In the following list I give examples of terms in conventional, Wade-Giles, Pinyin, and Yale forms. The Yale system is included as a teaching tool, not usually used in formal writing, which probably best assists English speakers in getting close to actual Chinese pronunciations. Note the similarity of the pinyin and Yale systems.

Conventional	Wade-Giles	Pinyin	Yale
Keelung	Chi-lung	Jilong	Jilung
Taipei	T'ai-pei	Taibei	Taibei
Kaohsiung	Kao-hsiung	Gaoxiong	Gaosyung
Chiang Kai-shek	Chiang Chieh-shih	Jiang Jieshi	Jiang Jyeshr
Sun Yat-sen	Sun I-hsien	Sun Yixian	Swun Yisyan

Certain renderings in pinyin do look strange to the English speaker. They have been chosen to represent double consonant sounds or to dramatize the fact that the sound is not easily pronounced by the English speaker. Examples of the strange-looking renderings are given in the following list, with comparisons to other romanization systems. Remember that the Yale system provides the best guide for relatively close pronunciation.

Pinyin	Wade-Giles	Yale
Qianlong	Ch'ien-lung	Chyanlung
Kangxi	K'ang-hsi	Kangsyi
cuo	ts'o	tswo

Also be aware that pinyin renders certain terms in such manner as to end with the letter *i*, when in fact the sound ending the word is close to the final *r* in English. Again, pay special attention to the Yale system in making the following comparisons.

Pinyin	Wade-Giles	Yale
shi	shih	shr
chi	ch'ih	chr
zhi	chih	jr

Chapter 1

TAIWAN BEFORE THE SEVENTEENTH CENTURY

Several thousand years before the Qin (221–206 B.C.) and Han (202 B.C.–A.D. 220) dynasties developed an enduring style of imperial rule on mainland China, the first inhabitants arrived on the island of Taiwan. The very first of these people came presumably from the Chinese mainland during the very distant and murky millennia of humankind's prehistory, destined to be absorbed by later arrivals. The origins of these later immigrants are a matter of ongoing anthropological and linguistic research. Some scholars trace their origins to Southeastern China; others maintain that they came to Taiwan from islands of Southeast Asia and the Pacific. In either case, their migrations had taken these people to Taiwan long before the Shang (ca. 1500–1000 B.C.) and Zhou (ca. 1000–246 B.C.) dynasties brought civilization to China. The later arrivals to Taiwan were the ancestors of today's *yuanzhumin,* the "original inhabitants" or aborigines. At least nine surviving aboriginal groups together constitute about 2 percent of Taiwan's current population of 23 million. The readily identifiable aboriginal groups include the Ami, Paiwan, Taya, Bunun, Puyuma, Rukai, Tsou, Yami, and Saisiat people. Two other groups, the Taroko and the Thao, are distinctive enough to expand the total number of discrete aboriginal groups in today's Taiwan to 11, under some schemes of classification.[1]

Taiwan's aborigines were among those Austronesian people, speaking a variety of Malayo-Polynesian dialects, who pursued courses that took them to such places as the Philippines, New Zealand, Australia, and the many islands of the Pacific Ocean. About 4000 B.C., some of these people settled in Taiwan. During the next 5,500 years or so, they and their descendants defined culture on Taiwan, building an economy based on horticulture, hunting, gathering, and fishing. They fashioned cord-marked pottery and sophisticated stone tools and, by 2500 B.C., produced digging sticks, stone knives, and hoes to aid them in planting millet and rice. The aborigines practiced the slash-and-burn or swidden style of agriculture common in Southeast Asia, eventually adding taro, yams, and sugarcane to their array of cultivated plants. They had no draft animals or plow agriculture, but they raised dogs, pigs, and chickens. Deer and wild boars fell to their bows and arrows, snares, and iron-tipped spears. Fish succumbed to their nets, basket traps, and derris poison.[2]

Taiwan's aborigines maintained contact with a variety of people from the Chinese mainland, Vietnam, Indonesia, and the Philippines. As the last centuries B.C. gave way to the first centuries A.D., the aborigines were producing iron in forges similar to those used in Indonesia. Wooden utensils carved with iron implements came to supplant ancient pottery forms. Borrowing another device from the people of Indonesia, the aborigines used the backstrap loom to produce distinctive woven goods.[3]

Similar patterns of social, cultural, and political organization may be noted among aboriginal groups of Taiwan during the many centuries in which contact with people of mainland China was minimal. The aborigines organized themselves into politically independent and self-sufficient villages featuring a highly egalitarian social structure. Kinship was an important principle of household and community organization, but units of association such as age grades and cult groups were also significant. Married couples were ideally monogamous. Nuclear or stem arrangements dominated among family residential units. Males did most of the hunting and fishing; during peak hunting seasons the primary hunters of the village lived together in quarters separate from the standard familial homes. Women dominated the gathering and cultivation of edible plants. Although Taiwan's aborigines recognized rights to individual and household property, land was not among the privately held commodities: It could not be traded or sold, and territorial demarcation was fluid. Certain lands—especially those immediately surrounding a village—were understood to be the special province of people from the village, but much territory was understood to be open to all for fishing, gathering, and hunting. Yet, the most physically vigorous inhabitants in the villages did often defend zones of security and primary usage. To take the head of an enemy brought much prestige in many of these aboriginal communities: Heads of decapitated foes hung on poles or rested on open outdoor shelves, giving evidence of an individual's or a village's success in armed conflict.[4]

Each of Taiwan's aboriginal groups produced distinctive housing styles, artistic motifs, types of personal ornamentation, village sizes, religious concepts, and languages. Although each language belonged to the Malayo-Polynesian family, most were incomprehensible to those aborigines who spoke another language in the family. In time, a distinction arose between plains aborigines and mountain aborigines. The plains groups depended more on agriculture and coastal fishing, whereas those who made their homes in the mountains of Taiwan turned chiefly to hunting, gathering, and riverine fishing for sustenance. In many cases, mountain aborigines who originally lived on the plains escaped to the highlands under pressure from more aggressive or militarily successful groups.[5]

Taiwan's aborigines dwelt on a stunningly beautiful island that stretches nearly 245 miles from northeast to southwest and approximately 90 miles from northwest to southeast. Mountains rise out of the sea on the east coast and run like a spine along the island's interior. A fertile plain covers most of western Taiwan, and good farmland also exists at the northern and southern extremes of Taiwan. Across the island, rainfall averages about 100 inches per year, with some regions receiving 200 inches some years. The north's rainiest season is winter; the south, more prone to meteorological vagaries and destruction from typhoons, gets most of its rain in the summer. In general, seasonal temperatures and humidity levels on Taiwan are similar to those of the Gulf Coast in the United States: Summer weather prevails from April to November, and the heart of summer features temperatures of 90 degrees Fahrenheit or more and high humidity. Temperatures drop from December through March to a mean of 59 degrees Fahrenheit, but the weather is never frigid.[6]

Taiwan emerged from the Pacific Ocean about a million years ago through geological processes similar to those that created the Japanese and Philippine archipelagos. Over thousands of years, lush grasses took root on the western plains, broad-leaved deciduous trees and conifers filled the forests, and 1,500 species of subtropical and tropical plants across the island contributed to Taiwan's beauty. Fauna such as Formosan black bears, foxes, flying foxes, wild boars, bats, squirrels, rabbits, deer, and many species of birds and insects pervaded the island. Several mountain peaks soared at 10,000 feet, and the highest point in Taiwan rose to 13,114 feet above sea level. Only at the highest elevations was snow likely to fall and linger on the terrain.[7]

The first credible evidence of Chinese contact with Taiwan comes from A.D. 239 when, after the fall of the great Han dynasty, the ruler of the southern Chinese kingdom of Wu sent a 10,000-soldier expeditionary force to explore the island. Migrants from the Chinese mainland braved the turbu-

lent Taiwan strait as early as the seventh century A.D., but the resulting settlement was tiny. At the beginning of the eleventh century (early in the
Song dynasty's rule), conditions of excess population and economic difficulty led many in China to seek a better life outside its borders, beyond the
authority of the dynastic government. Among the first to pursue this route,
the severely strapped farmers and fishers of the Quanzhou area in Fujian,
found their way to Penghu, as did a smattering of pirates and political
refugees. During the thirteenth and fourteenth centuries, representatives of
the Mongols' Yuan dynasty took control of Penghu. They installed a circuit
intendant there, thus establishing the first Chinese imperial claim on the
Taiwan area.[8]

Ming dynasty officials did their best to arrest any nascent tendency of
southern Chinese to make their way to Taiwan. Strict prohibitions forbade
coastal people to leave their native land; and, in an effort to root out Japanese pirates, the emperor decreed that Chinese should not sail into ocean
waters for fishing or trade. Those who crossed to Penghu did so as outlaws.
The government became increasingly concerned as Penghu became a
gathering place for pirates and immigrants who threw in their lot with the
"dwarf bandits" (an epithet the Chinese frequently used to refer to the Japanese). In time the government closed the sixth circuit government office
on Penghu and decreed that all those living on Penghu return to Fujian; but
the immigrants just bribed officials, sought further help from pirates, and
kept coming to Penghu. They also came increasingly to Taiwan. Pirates
such as Lin Daogan, Lin Feng, Yan Siji, Lin Dan, and Zheng Zhilong controlled the Taiwan Straits, occupied Taiwan, and managed the waves of
immigrants. In 1628 Zheng accepted the Ming court's appointment to help
defend the dynasty from the invading Manchus; in exchange, Zheng was
expected to curb his piratical activities, impede the raids of other pirates,
and enforce the ban on migration to Penghu. But as the Ming rulers succumbed to Manchu invaders, who in 1644 inaugurated the new Qing
dynasty, immigrants made their way to the island in increasing numbers.[9]

Into the seventeenth century, then, assertion of Chinese mainland power
was limited, unenduring and lacked sustained interest. Chinese settlement
was focused in a few small pockets of agrarian, mercantile, and piratical
activity. The aborigines still overwhelmingly dominated the population.
Not until the mid-seventeenth century, under pressure from Europeans'
arrival in coastal Asia and from Manchu efforts to quell the resistance of
Ming loyalists in South China, did a Chinese imperial administration manifest a greater political interest in Taiwan. During the early to middle
decades of the seventeenth century, contention for power on the island

took place not between the Chinese and Manchus but between Spanish and Dutch traders, who regarded the island's strategic and economic value as consonant with their imperialist interests. By pursuing those interests in Asian waters, they followed a course first undertaken by the Portuguese.[10]

From the late sixteenth century, Taiwan was targeted by colonizers. Portugal was the first nation to sail all-water routes from Europe, around the southern tip of Africa, to Asia. The Portuguese established a base on Macao in 1557 and passed by Taiwan on their expeditions. (In fact, an adaptation of *Ilha Formosa* or "Beautiful Island," the Portuguese name for Taiwan, became the name that most Europeans used for the island well into the twentieth century: Formosa.) In 1571 the Spaniards occupied Manila; soon the Taiwan strait was full of European ships. The mainland Chinese rulers of the Ming dynasty considered China to be economically self-sufficient and thus repeatedly refused Portuguese and Spanish requests for trading privileges. These European countries, as well as Japan, developed designs on Taiwan, each unsuccessfully scheming to occupy the island. Great Britain and the Netherlands followed these nations into East Asia and eventually forced Portugal and Spain to evacuate many trading posts. In 1604 the Dutch occupied Penghu but were forced by Ming official Shen Yourong to retreat. On July 27, 1622, the Dutch explored the deepwater coast of southwestern Taiwan, the first such arrival recorded for Europeans.[11]

Later that same year, the Dutch returned, full of ambitions for Taiwan and giving evidence of a willingness to use force in pursuit of their ambitions. They confiscated 600 fishing vessels and commandeered the labor of 1,500 Chinese who by that time had migrated to Penghu; the labor went mainly toward erecting fortifications to protect the budding Dutch interest. The Dutch went about their business with notable harshness, allotting the laborers only a half-*jin* (catty) of rice per day; before the fortifications were complete, 1,300 Chinese had died from starvation. Those lucky enough to survive were shipped as slave laborers to Indonesia. In 1624 the governor of Fujian led an attack on Baisha ("White Sand") Island of the Penghu group, surrounded the Dutch fortifications there, and captured the Dutch general defending the outpost. There then ensued an eight-month war before the Dutch agreed to peace terms calling for them to give up Penghu. The Dutch moved to nearby Taiwan without Ming dynasty objection; accordingly, the Dutch destroyed their Penghu battlements, turned their attentions to Taiwan, and began erecting Fort Zeelandia, at the location that would come to be known by the Chinese as Anping, on August 26, 1624. For the next 40 years the Dutch would exercise colonial rule on the island.[12]

At first, Dutch rule was contested by the Spaniards, whose government had already laid claim to the Philippines. A Dutch base so near the main Spanish holding in the Asian-Pacific region created a state of alarm among authorities in the Philippines. In 1627 the Spanish authorities dispatched an armed force to the northeast corner of Taiwan, laying claim to the region and naming it San Tiago. They occupied the area encompassing today's Jilong (Keelung), giving it the name San Salvador. In the area of today's Tasha Bay they established a settlement in which they encouraged residence by Han Chinese. In 1629 the Spaniards erected the fort of San Domingo in the area today known as Danshui (Tamsui). Perceiving a threat to their own interests on Taiwan, the Dutch sent naval forces northward along the western coast. Many years of war ensued with neither side able to dislodge the other from its base area. But in 1642 the Spaniards, smarting from recent losses to the Dutch, plagued by attacks from the aborigines, and reevaluating the necessity of holding onto their northern Taiwan strong-hold, elected to abandon Fort San Domingo, reduce fortifications at Jilong (San Salvador), board their ships, and give up any sustained effort to compete with the Dutch on Taiwan. Soon the Spaniards abandoned the Jilong fortifications, conceding control of both northern and southern Taiwan to the Dutch, who soon exclusively controlled the carrying trade from Taiwan to China and Japan.[13]

No Chinese imperial administration had yet placed Taiwan on a map of Chinese territory. Those who left for Taiwan did so illegally and of their own accord, placing themselves beyond the pale of Chinese protection. Chinese governments traditionally frowned upon emigration from the mainland. Officially, they saw those who departed China and thus left the Confucian "Way of the Enlightened Ruler" as having moved outside the borders of civilization. Clear evidence of this disdain for emigrants surfaced during an ugly incident in 1603, when Spanish authorities on Luzon killed 23,000 Han Chinese who had settled in the Philippines. In response, the circuit intendant of Fujian (following a directive of the imperial court) sent a callous communication to the Spanish viceroy of the Philippines: "Those who reside in foreign lands have all abandoned their native places in pursuit of monetary gain: Accordingly, they are a debased form of humanity for whom our protection is unnecessary."[14]

Governments of the emperors had similarly looked with contempt on any Chinese who made their way to Taiwan. Only when Taiwan became a nuisance as a pirate's lair did the Chinese court give the island any notice at all. In any case, the beleaguered rulers of the Ming dynasty in the mid-seventeenth century were in no position to concern themselves much with the Han Chinese people living under Dutch rule. But one Ming loyalist's need for a base of operations to withstand pressure from the Manchus—and the Manchus' interest in pursuing this holdout against their rule—eventually stimulated greater interest in the fate of Taiwan by the imperial dynasty of China.

NOTES

1. Zhou Mingfeng, *Taiwan jian shi* [A concise history of Taiwan] (Taibei: Qian Wei Press, 1994), p. 15; Miyamoto Nobehito, *Taiwan di yuanzhu minzu* [The original inhabitants of Taiwan], trans. Wei Guibang (Taibei: Chenxing Press, 1992), p. 68. For a concise summary of the evidence and the political overtones associated with aborigine origins, see Michael Stainton, "The Politics of Taiwan Aborigine Origins," in Murray A. Rubinstein, ed., *Taiwan: A New History* (Armonk, New York: M. E. Sharpe, 1999).

2. John Robert Shepherd, *Statecraft and Political Economy on the Taiwan Frontier* (Stanford, Calif.: Stanford University Press, 1993), pp. 20–29; Gary Marvin Davison and Barbara E. Reed, *Culture and Customs of Taiwan* (Westport, Conn.: Greenwood Press, 1998), p. 4.

3. Shepherd, p. 29; Davison and Reed, pp. 4–5.

4. Shepherd, pp. 30–32; Davison and Reed, p. 5; Chen Kang Chai, *Taiwan Aborigines: A Genetic Study of Tribal Variations* (Cambridge, Mass.: Harvard University Press, 1967), pp. 38–48.

5. Shepherd, pp. 30–32; Davison and Reed, pp. 5–6.

6. John F. Copper, *Taiwan: Nation-State or Province?* (Boulder, Colo.: Westview, 1990), p. 5; Department of Agriculture and Forestry, *Taiwan Agricultural Yearbook* (Taichung, Taiwan: Department of Agriculture and Forestry, Taiwan Provincial Government, 1990), pp. 336–37; Davison and Reed, p. 2.

7. Copper, p. 2; Davison and Reed, pp. 3–4.

8. Copper, pp. 18–19; Davison and Reed, p. 6.

9. Qi Jialin, *Taiwan shi* [The history of Taiwan], vol. 1 (Taibei: Zili Evening News, 1985), pp. 27–28; Zhou Mingfeng, p. 17.

10. Zhou Mingfeng, p. 19.

11. Ibid., pp. 17–19; Huang Dashou, *Taiwan shi gang* [An outline history of Taiwan] (Taibei: Sanmin Book Company, 1982), p. 37.

12. Zhou Mingfeng, pp. 18–19; Huang Dashou, pp. 37–40; Qi Jialin, pp. 1–11.

13. Zhou Mingfeng, pp. 19–20; Huang Dashou, pp. 56–58; Qi Jialin, pp. 19–24.

14. Zhou Mingfeng, p. 20.

Chapter 2

DUTCH COLONIAL RULE, 1624–61

Not until 1579 did the Dutch throw off Spanish rule, establish the Dutch Republic, and embark on a century of commercial and imperial dynamism out of proportion with the home country's size. The Dutch allied with the British, and together the Netherlands and Great Britain ended the oceangoing domination of Portugal and Spain. In 1602 the Dutch East India Company was founded, and the Dutch oceangoing empire established headquarters in Batavia, capital of the Dutch imperial claim in the East Indies (today's Indonesia). From this base of operations, the Dutch funneled supplies to and received goods from Taiwan and launched forays to Japan and elsewhere in East Asia. After setting up on Taiwan, the Dutch soon came to comprehend the favorable agricultural conditions and latent potential for economic growth there. To exploit the economic potential of the island, the colonial government stationed 600 officials on Taiwan, backed by 2,000 troops. These were immediately put to work erecting fortifications, producing the chief forts of Zeelandia (at coastal Anping, ready in 1632), and Provintia (in the heart of today's Tainan, completed in 1650).[1]

The Dutch used Fort Provintia to expand their territorial hold on southern Taiwan, clearing fields for establishing farms in the Chinese style, with the use of Chinese labor. This of course meant encroaching upon lands used by the aborigines in their hunting and agricultural activities. The aborigines fought back repeatedly and fiercely, most vigorously in 1635 during the Great Matou Resistance, in which the aborigines of Matou north of

Tainan rebelled against the Dutch authorities. In the end, though, bows and arrows were no match for Dutch guns and artillery. The colonial forces slaughtered hundreds of thousands of aborigines. Within 10 years the Dutch occupied the entire southwestern plain, having brought most of the resisters among the plains aborigines under control. Any unyielding or stubbornly fierce opposition fled to the mountains and other areas not yet occupied by the Dutch. In this process of suppression, the population of the plains aborigines had been cut in half, from 600,000 at the beginning of Dutch rule to 300,000 by the late 1630s.[2]

As they suppressed the aborigines militarily, the Dutch sought to convert them spiritually. In 1627 the Calvinist Dutch Reformed Church dispatched Georgius Candidius to Xingang, near Tainan, thus beginning the effort to spread Christianity to the aborigines. Two years later, Robertus Junius joined Candidius in the effort. In all, 30 Dutch missionaries came to Taiwan. They used romanized spellings to compose a Bible and a dictionary in the languages of the aborigines in the Xingang area. In all, they baptized 6,000 aborigines. The Dutch also established schools, inculcating in some aboriginal folk an understanding of Western learning. Such a policy resulted in the acculturation of a good many aborigines, who were induced to do the bidding of the Dutch in administrative and military matters, including the quelling of the occasional revolt of Han Chinese.[3]

Needing a large-scale labor force to prepare previously uncultivated fields and manage new sugarcane and rice farms, the Dutch turned to the agriculturally experienced, hardworking Han Chinese. During the late years of Ming rule, even before the Dutch took control of Taiwan, the pirate and trader Zheng Zhilong had run a lucrative transport operation carting to Taiwan many desperate Chinese who sought to escape the poverty and starvation of southern China. Not only did the Dutch allow Zheng to continue his activities; they even began using their own Dutch East India Company ships to transport Chinese emigrating from the Fujianese districts of Quanzhou and Zhangzhou in particular. All the land that the Chinese worked was classified as "King's Lands," officially possessed by the monarch of the Netherlands. The lands produced considerable revenue for the Dutch administration, which reaped the yield of the land through various tax schemes: head tax, customs duties, commodity tax, "barbarian" trade tax, fishing tax, hunting tax, sulfur extraction tax, and liquor brewing tax.[4]

Han Chinese had long traded rice, salt, and textiles for the specialty goods of Taiwan, most especially deer hides and preserved venison. When the Dutch took control of Taiwan and monopolized its trade, they carried deer hides from the island to Japan and traded preserved venison to Fujian. As agricultural production increased, the Dutch found a lucrative market for sugarcane in Japan and traded rice to China. The Dutch also supplied Cambodia and China with sulfur (used in the production of gunpowder) from the mines of northern Taiwan. The Dutch shipped Chinese silks (both raw and finished), pottery, and porcelain for sale back in the Netherlands. Fort Zeelandia at Anping served as the way station for exchange and retransport in the Dutch-controlled trade. Since the pirate-trader Zheng Zhilong operated and exercised considerable power in the Taiwan strait and on the East and South China Seas, the Dutch three times concluded trade agreements with him. For a time the Dutch were preeminent on the seas of East Asia, making Taiwan a most important base of operations.[5]

One of those who assisted Zheng Zhilong in his transport operation was a man named Guo Huaiyi. About the time that Zheng Zhilong was accepting appointment in the service of the fading Ming dynasty, Guo led more than 2,000 people to Taiwan for the purpose of opening additional land to cultivation. Guo resented the ironclad, arrogant rule of the Dutch and their many economic exactions. On September 7, 1652, Guo gathered his supporters together at his home, plied them generously with liquor, and raised their own anti-Dutch sentiments to a fever pitch. He outlined a plan whereby Dutch officials would be invited to an evening feast in anticipation of the Mid-Autumn Festival; in a classic ruse found often in tales from Chinese history, these Dutch officials would, if the plan held, fall victim to murder at the hands of Guo's supporters. Guo's subordinates would then rush Fort Provintia and seize this bastion of Dutch rule on Taiwan.[6]

Local strongman Pu Zai and a younger brother of Guo Huaiyi foiled the plan. They panicked and revealed the scheme to the Dutch. When Guo discovered this, he moved precipitously on Fort Provintia, investing 16,000 troops in the effort, slaughtering well over a thousand Dutch, and setting the fort ablaze. The following day the Dutch assembled a force of 120 armed troops along the western shore of the Tai River; several days later, 2,000 aborigines came to the assistance of the Dutch, launching a vigorous attack. The Chinese immigrant force had little time to prepare adequately and typically raised only hoes and bamboo poles along with a paltry number of firearms. Guo fell along with 1,800 other settlers. Guo's second in command was captured and burned to death, his corpse paraded in the streets, his head severed and carried about on a bamboo pole. Additionally, two brigade leaders suffered the indignity of being drawn and quartered.[7]

Leaderless, the rebel Chinese retreated to their home base. Aborigines doing the bidding of the Dutch crossed the Tai River in pursuit, caught up with the Chinese forces, and for seven bloody days and nights inflicted and sustained great harm: While Chinese dropped all around them, 10,000 aborigine fighters also went to their deaths. In the end, the combination of the initial treachery, inadequate preparation, the launch of a hasty attack on Fort Provintia, other farmers' failure to join the rebellion, and the willingness of the aborigines to serve the Dutch effort doomed the Guo Huaiyi Rebellion.[8]

This propensity to rebel against externally imposed authority became a notable feature of Taiwanese history; the annals of the island are replete with such incidents in this frontier society. Other enduring themes in Taiwan's history can be seen as early as the Dutch period of control. One of these themes, economic competition between the aborigines and the Han, was often exploited by external rulers who played one group against the other. Yet this contentiousness of life on the frontier, in large measure traceable to ethnic and subethnic tensions, would also be a giant headache to external authorities seeking to stabilize their rule.[9]

Under the Dutch, Han Chinese immigrants gradually adapted to the particular environment of Taiwan. Though ethnic tension was an abiding reality on the island, some Han Chinese became friendly with aboriginal people, learned their languages, and intermarried with them. Amid the resultant complex range of possible interactions from friendly to contentious, the coexistence of aborigine and Han Chinese people became an enduring feature of Taiwanese society, a part of what it meant to be Taiwanese. Many Taiwanese learned something of the larger international forces that governed their economic production, gaining knowledge of concepts pertinent to mercantilism and to commercialized rather than self-sufficient agriculture. In time some people would leave the farm to expand family economies in thriving port communities along the western coast of Taiwan. As Taiwan's economy became linked to international trade, entrepreneurs and traders would gather in these port towns, giving the Taiwanese economy a distinct mercantile sector to complement the primary sector of agriculture. This orientation toward the sea, with an awareness of the economic opportunities afforded by international trade, also became part of the mix of features that would define the Taiwanese people.[10]

Over the long course of history preceding the seventeenth century, Taiwan lay almost totally outside the scope of imperial Chinese interest. But during that century, events spawned by the Manchu invasion of China and defeat of the faltering Ming dynasty brought representatives of the Chinese empire more insistently into the story of the Taiwanese past. The vigorous but ultimately unsuccessful efforts of a son of the pirate-trader

Zheng Zhilong to turn back the Manchu tide in southern China would eventually send him scrambling for a safe haven. He chose Taiwan, thus opening another chapter in the history of the island's fascinating and unique people.

NOTES

1. Zhou Mingfeng, *Taiwan jian shi* [A concise history of Taiwan] (Taibei: Qian Wei Press, 1994), pp. 23–24; Huang Dashou, *Taiwan shi gang* [An outline history of Taiwan] (Taibei: Sanmin Book Company, 1982), pp. 43–46; Qi Jialin, *Taiwan shi* [The history of Taiwan], vol. 1 (Taibei: Zili Evening News, 1985), pp. 11–13.

2. Zhou Mingfeng, p. 25; Huang Dashou, pp. 47–52.

3. Zhou Mingfeng, pp. 25–26; Huang Dashou, pp. 63–64; Qi Jialin, pp. 48–49.

4. Zhou Mingfeng, pp. 26–27; Huang Dashou, pp. 62–63; Qi Jialin, pp. 30–32.

5. Zhou Mingfeng, pp. 24–25; Huang Dashou, pp. 58–60; Qi Jialin, pp. 34–43.

6. Zhou Mingfeng, pp. 28–29; Qi Jialin, p. 42.

7. Zhou Mingfeng, p. 29; Qi Jialin, pp. 42–43.

8. Zhou Mingfeng, pp. 29–30; Qi Jialin, pp. 42–43.

9. Zhou Mingfeng, p. 30.

10. John Robert Shepherd, *Statecraft and Political Economy on the Taiwan Frontier* (Stanford, Calif.: Stanford University Press, 1993), pp. 28–29.

Chapter 3

ZHENG FAMILY RULE, 1661–83

By the mid-seventeenth century the powerful elite among the Manchus, positioned to the northeast of China proper, had developed a strong desire to seize control of East Asia's great empire. Events in the early 1640s gave them the opportunity they sought. A dissident seized control of the Chinese capital, Beijing, chasing the Ming court from the city and precipitating the suicide of the last Ming emperor. In 1644 Manchu armies responded to the invitation of another rebel against the Ming to join him in ousting his rival from Beijing. The Manchus eagerly swept through the Shanhaiguan Pass and quickly established themselves as North China's strongest force. Defeating some rivals and co-opting others, the Manchus took control of the North with limited bloodshed. Their Qing dynasty (1644–1912) became one of the most enduring dynasties to rule the essential territory that comprises today's China proper, and its governance of the empire would encompass a remarkable period during which the people of a self-satisfied Middle Kingdom were forced to come to terms with European-engineered modernity.[1]

Though the Manchus had gained control of North China with little difficulty, the South would prove more of a challenge. There, as Ming rulers began to lose their grip on the various regions of China, bandits crisscrossed the land and great disorder prevailed. Through the Manchus' efforts to bring southern China under their control, the histories of mainland China and Taiwan come to be more intimately interwoven. Fujianese strongman Zheng Zhilong fell in one Manchu incursion into the South;

this defeat of Zheng, whose talents and influence had impressed the rulers of the Ming and the colonial regime of the Dutch, posed a huge challenge to the resistance movement in the crucial Jiangnan area of China. Zheng Zhilong's son, Zheng Chenggong, took up the challenge.[2]

Born in Fujian province, Zheng Chenggong had in his early years been raised in Japan by the family of his Chinese father's Japanese wife. He was brought back to his native Fujian at the age of seven and eventually became steeped in the political manipulations of his canny father. When Zheng Zhilong supported the Ming loyalists as part of his own strategy for remaining powerful in South China, a then 20-year-old Zheng Chenggong himself achieved numerous military exploits for the cause. The last Ming emperor bestowed upon the younger Zheng the title of *Guo xingye,* the European pronunciation of which gave rise to the alternate name found in many histories: Koxinga. After Zheng Zhilong fell to the forces of the Qing, his son raised the flag of resistance and embraced the slogan "Resist the Qing; Restore the Ming." He gathered his forces on the islands of Kulangsu, Jinmen (Quemoy), and Xiamen (Amoy) off the Fujian coast and for a time orchestrated many a failed incursion. Then, in 1658, Zheng Chenggong's forces mounted a highly significant challenge to the Manchu forces of South China. They captured the Jiangsu provincial capital of Zhenjiang and surrounded the most important southern city, Nanjing. Nanjing had served as the capital of all China during the early years of the Ming dynasty and continued to function as a kind of dual capital. But in a familiar motif of Chinese history, the threat of these challengers conducting a siege of Nanjing faltered amid military miscalculation, indecision, and loss of nerve. Having failed to seize the moment, Zheng was forced to retreat southward to Jinmen and Xiamen. Zheng maintained a significant following but needed a new base of operations. With the Manchus tightening their control over South China, Dutch-controlled Taiwan seemed an island of logical location and adequate size for reestablishing his resistance efforts.[3]

Meanwhile, the Dutch had established firm control over the southwestern coastal areas of Taiwan. Anti-Dutch sentiment increased among the Han Chinese population after the Guo Huaiyi Rebellion had come to its brutal end, and the events of southern China seemed to the Dutch rulers to point toward Taiwan as an area likely coveted by the Ming resistance forces. Faced with these dual trouble spots for their rule, the colonial regime on Taiwan requested reinforcements from the Dutch East India Company headquarters in Batavia. As this request was being tendered, a Chinese interpreter and arbitrator by the name of He Bin defected and escaped with a haul from the Dutch treasury. He made his way to Xiamen, where he presented a map and geographical analysis of Taiwan to Zheng Chenggong. The resources acquired through He Bin's defection bolstered the intention of Zheng and his followers to defeat the Dutch and bring Taiwan under their control.[4]

Zheng Chenggong had seemingly inherited the craftiness of his father in creating maximally beneficial conditions for his own initiatives. He cultivated good relations with the Dutch, scaled down their suspicions, and waited patiently for them to reduce the naval forces guarding the island. He waited until the Dutch East India Company decided that a large fleet guarding Taiwan could be more usefully employed in other pursuits; then he launched an all-out assault on the island. On April 23, 1661, Zheng led 25,000 troops in an attack on Penghu, seized the main strategic points of these islands, and, with He Bin charting the course, moved on Taiwan. He Bin led the forces to the mouth of the Tai River, through the Luermen Waterway between Laowan and Beixianwei islands off the southwestern Taiwan coast, and landed at the port of Heliao on April 30. Soon these forces had seized control of Fort Provintia and surrounded Fort Zeelandia. Here, Zheng's soldiers were forced to settle in for a siege that lasted several months before it broke the Dutch will. Even as the decisive final days of Dutch control unfolded, Dutch commander Frederik Coyett gave up control of Anping only very hesitantly. He tendered one surrender offer and then decided to hold out for the arrival of reinforcements, which did in fact arrive but met with defeat in a series of bloody battles. The Dutch took stock of 1,600 troop casualties over more than seven months of bitter battle. With conviction this time, they sought terms of surrender. On February 12, 1662, the Dutch evacuated Taiwan and said good-bye to a rule that had lasted 38 years. Zheng Chenggong formally assumed power on Taiwan. The rule that he and his family established on Taiwan from 1662 to 1684 deepened the Qing rulers' interest in the island. The necessity that the Manchus perceived in ending the rule of the Zheng family on Taiwan took on momentous importance in the island's unique history.[5]

After Zheng Chenggong took control on Taiwan, he designated the area around the fort of Anping as Anping Zhen (formerly Fort Zeelandia), gave the name of Chengtian Fu to the area lying near Chikan fort (formerly Fort Provintia), and collectively called the territory encompassing these two forts the Eastern Capital (*Dong du*). He also established the *xian* (county) of Tianxing and Wannian and installed a pacification official on Penghu. He enforced a severe legal code and forcefully subjugated the aborigines within his governing sphere. Zheng created military farms, employing soldiers in farming and land reclamation, and he oversaw the expansion of foreign trade. In all, Zheng Chenggong ruled Taiwan for 14 months; he passed away on June 23, 1662, at the age of 39. Upon his death, a group of admirers organized a campaign to fund the building of a shrine in his honor. The shrine, dedicated to the *Kaishan wang* ("the king who opened the way for pioneers in the mountains"), endures to this day, although it underwent numerous name changes and political uses as different external regimes established themselves on Taiwan.[6]

Zheng Chenggong's son, Zheng Jing, succeeded his father as ruler of Taiwan. More accurately, Zheng Jing ruled an area extending from today's Tainan City and County to the midpoint of Taiwan's western coast, for no Zheng ever achieved anything close to complete control over the island's aborigines, and Han Chinese settlement only slowly moved northward. Ten years into Zheng Jing's rule, the Manchus continued to battle anti-Qing forces in South China, with two notable campaigns taking place in 1673: a struggle with the famous Three Feudatories and the revolt of Geng Jingzhong in Fujian. Geng sought the aid of Zheng Jing, who responded by leaving his aide Chen Yonghua to guard Taiwan as Zheng himself led a large force to the mainland. Zheng succeeded in bringing seven administrative districts of Fujian under his control and also secured Jinmen and Xiamen as anti-Qing redoubts. Ultimately, though, the Manchu forces proved too strong for the challengers. Geng Jingzhong met defeat, and by 1680 Zheng himself had been worn down by the forces of the Qing. He died in 1681, completing a 19-year reign, nearly half of which he spent doing battle on the mainland.[7]

Yet Zheng Jing had put his own stamp on life in Taiwan. He changed the name Eastern Capital *(Dong du)* to Eastern Peace *(Dongning)*. He elevated the Anping and Chikan areas to the status of *zhou,* the administrative unit just above the county level in traditional Chinese terminology. He established aborigine pacification agencies on the main road running south to north along the western coast and on Penghu. Drawing upon Chen Yonghua's talent for strategic planning, Zheng opened up more and more land to cultivation, worked to promote handicraft production, encouraged trade, and increased economic exploitation of Taiwan's forests. Zheng also embraced the fundamental ideas and institutions of traditional Chinese education and bureaucracy. He established a Confucian temple, founded schools, sponsored exams for the evaluation of prospective government officials, and sponsored a study that yielded a plan for long-term education on Taiwan. Zheng Chenggong had defeated the Dutch and established his family in a position of power on the island, but it was his son Zheng Jing whose policies resulted in government effective enough to keep the Zheng family in power for more than two decades.[8]

Zheng family rulers continued to observe a calendar based on Ming dynasty beginnings and proceeded with policies designed to build up resources to a level of surplus sufficient to fund future military offensives against the Qing. The new rulers of Taiwan built upon Dutch institutions in establishing their own administration. Having inherited the King's Lands system, the Zheng family opted not to return these lands to the farmers but to claim them for themselves. The policy of the Zheng administration was to establish a militia system to open up new lands for cultivation so as to supply the army with foodstuffs. The administration also established the Officials' Lands system of newly cultivated fields for the Zheng family and its military and civilian officials. Ordinary farmers cultivated only enough land to minimally clothe and feed themselves. The lot of the common farmer was at least as tough under the Zheng family as it had been under the Dutch.[9]

In the days when the Manchu forces were pressing in upon Zheng Chenggong and precipitating his flight to Taiwan, the Qing court had proclaimed sea prohibitions and boundary removal orders. These orders severely restricted the seagoing activities of residents along the coast of southeastern China and eventually required them to abandon their home villages for locations lying 10 to 17 miles inland. Buildings in the coastal villages were burned to the ground, forcing villagers into refugee status. Zheng Chenggong sent representatives to areas along the Fujian and Guangdong coasts to aid the refugees and transport those who wanted to come to Taiwan. Those braving the seas increased steadily; estimates place the Han Chinese population of Taiwan at 150,000 to 200,000 by the end of the Zheng period.[10]

Some of these settlers came to Taiwan with the intent to stay temporarily; they hoped to return to the mainland when life in China stabilized after the dislocations of the Ming-Qing transition. This sense of Taiwan as a temporary location was even greater among Zheng Chenggong and his supporters. The Zheng family dispelled the Dutch and occupied Taiwan so as to establish a base for overthrowing the Qing and restoring the Ming. The family established a militarized rule on the island and exerted great efforts toward territorial confiscation, resource extraction, and military conscription. The Zheng rulers called for a great deal of physical sacrifice from the people they ruled, engendering significant loss of life in the ill-considered attempt to aid anti-Qing forces in Fujian. Ironically, Zheng Jing built his army operating in South China in such manner that, although many conscripts from Taiwan died, recruits who returned with him from the mainland exceeded the number he had taken with him. The population increased 40 percent, placing more demands on the agricultural economy.[11]

When Zheng Jing took up the struggle in Fujian, he entrusted the defense of Taiwan to Chen Yonghua and established his eldest son, Zheng Kesang, as the island's acting governor. Zheng Kesang, who happened to be Chen's son-in-law, was bright and capable but did not get much of a chance to rule as the island's official governor. Chen died soon after Zheng Jing's demise; and with his key military support gone, Zheng Kesang fell victim to rumor mongering bodyguards who forced him to retire and ultimately killed him. Power then fell into the hands of Feng Xifan, father-in-law and regent to Zheng Jing's second son, Zheng Keshuang. Zheng Keshuang—only 12 years old—and regent Feng Xifan inspired little faith among the people, creating an unsettled political situation. In June 1683, when Qing naval captain Du Shi Lang attacked Penghu, those in charge of the institutions of Zheng family power had reason for grave concern. Liu Guxuan, the official charged with defense of Penghu, took up the struggle, which raged fiercely for seven days. The Zheng family loyalists led by Liu were defeated, a turn of events that increased the panic level among the Zheng regime's supporters on Taiwan. With confidence and morale very low, the fighting spirit dissipated. Those acting in behalf of the hapless young ruler Zheng Keshuang negotiated for surrender, issuing an official request for permission to retain their titles of nobility. Their hopes of maintaining some semblance of government status and official dignity died, though, when the Zheng court was forced to accept terms of unconditional surrender. All court officials evacuated Taiwan, and all political and military officials of the defunct regime moved to the mainland. Officials representing the Qing dynasty of the Manchus replaced those of the Zheng government on August 22, 1683, ending 23 years of Zheng family rule of Taiwan.[12]

By this time there had emerged a Han Chinese populace of individuals and some families who were firmly dedicated to remaining on Taiwan and making a new life for themselves. For decades to come, some inhabitants of Taiwan would seek to return to the mainland, but their numbers decreased with each passing year. Those Han Chinese already on Taiwan, together with those who came in subsequent decades despite the best efforts of the Qing to restrict immigration, came to feel an intense identification with the villages, temples, and subethnic groups that made up their immediate social universe. Contact with and memory of the mainland became more tenuous; for many people on Taiwan, knowledge of life on the mainland came to them through reports from recent immigrants, stories passed down in family lore, and traditions maintained through religious organizations. Fujian or Guangdong became a component of their heritage, but Taiwan was the abiding reality encompassing their families, economic endeavors, and evolving traditions. For the people on Taiwan increasingly identifying with life on the island, the officials of the Qing were rulers, nothing more. They were alternately tolerated and resisted, but loyalty to these representatives of mainland Chinese political authority was ever a matter of current circumstance, not of ongoing commitment on the part of the Taiwanese people. And once the Qing rulers convinced themselves that Taiwan was by a small margin worth possessing and governing, they remained a rather remote and aloof group to the people whose lives were actually firmly embedded in the conditions of community life on the island.[13] This tenuous and often contentious relationship between the Taiwanese people and the representatives of imperial China lies at the heart of the next chapter in the history of Taiwan.

NOTES

1. Qi Jialin, *Taiwan shi* [The history of Taiwan], vol. 1 (Taibei: Zili Evening News, 1985), pp. 143–44; Jonathon Spence, *The Search for Modern China* (New York: W. W. Norton & Company, 1990), pp. 31–38.

2. Zhou Mingfeng, *Taiwan jian shi* [A concise history of Taiwan] (Taibei: Qian Wei Press, 1994), pp. 31–32; Huang Dashou, *Taiwan shi gang* [An outline history of Taiwan] (Taibei: Sanmin Book Company, 1982), pp. 69–72.

3. Zhou Mingfeng, pp. 31–32; Qi Jialin, pp. 66–68. Huang Dashou discusses the family circumstances of Zheng Chenggong on pp. 66–68. On pp. 72–74 he provides a summary of the northern expedition that Zheng led to Nanjing.

4. Zhou Mingfeng, p. 32; Qi Jialin, pp. 66–69. On the wariness with which the Dutch regarded Zheng Chenggong, see Huang Dashou, pp. 73–78.

5. Zhou Mingfeng, pp. 32–33; Huang Dashou, pp. 78–86. On pp. 69–85, Qi Jialin gives a detailed summary of the entire period between the arrival of the forces led by Zheng on Taiwan in April 1661 and their final ousting of the Dutch in January 1662.

6. Zhou Mingfeng, pp. 33–34. Qi Jialin, on p. 117, discusses the circumstances of Zheng Chenggong's death. Huang Dashou, on pp. 86–91, discusses aspects of Zheng Chenggong's administration on Taiwan, the rapidity with which his health declined upon assuming rule of the island, and his passing of the mantle of leadership to son Zheng Jing.

7. Zhou Mingfeng, pp. 34–35; Huang Dashou, pp. 91–94. Qi Jialin discusses Zheng Jing's anti-Manchu activities on pp. 121–27 and on p. 129 discusses the events that transpired at Zheng Jing's death.

8. Zhou Mingfeng, pp. 34–35; Huang Dashou, pp. 94–100.

9. Zhou Mingfeng, pp. 36–38. Qi Jialin, on pp. 86–99, discusses the Zheng administration's agricultural and taxation policies in some detail.

10. Zhou Mingfeng, pp. 38–39; Qi Jialin, pp. 89–94. On p. 92, Qi Jialin has some particularly poignant passages from eyewitness accounts of tragic experiences resulting from the quarantine policies.

11. Zhou Mingfeng, on pp. 37–38, offers interesting commentary questioning the status of Zheng Chenggong as a hero.

12. Zhou Mingfeng, pp. 34–35; Huang Dashou, pp. 101–6.

13. Zhou Mingfeng, p. 41.

Chapter 4

QING DYNASTY RULE,
1684–1895

Virtually all prominent officials at the Qing court advised the emperor to abandon Taiwan to the aborigines. Many officials advocated the forcible return of all Han Chinese residing on Taiwan to their mainland communities in Fujian and Guangdong, after which the island and its inhabitants would be inconsequential. After all, the island had never been governed by any previous dynasty. The overwhelmingly dominant view was that incorporating Taiwan into the Qing realm held no significant advantage but numerous liabilities. Chinese officials viewed Taiwan as a wild and difficult place where robbers and fugitives from the law sought safe harbor. Many chief advisers to the Qing emperor considered Taiwan unworthy to be entered onto the map of the Middle Kingdom. One official described Taiwan as "a peripheral little mud ball, insufficient to significantly expand Chinese territory, a desolate and essentially uninhabited place, untouched by the wonder of the celestial deities."[1] An island that had been considered a valuable colonial property by the Dutch regime, and by the Zheng rulers an agriculturally productive safe haven to support a vision of military comeback on the mainland, was to most Qing advisers more trouble than it was worth.

Shi Lang, the fine scholar-official who had led the victory over the Zheng regime, was a notable exception at the Qing court. In a cogently argued memorial to the emperor, he maintained that Taiwan was strategically situated to protect the four provinces (Fujian, Jiangxi, Zhejiang, and Jiangsu) of the mainland Southeast. If the dynasty abandoned Taiwan and Penghu, he wrote, these islands would become beacons to pirates and other troublemakers seeking a hideout. Evacuating Taiwan and Penghu would also serve as an invitation to the Dutch to recover what they had lost two decades earlier. Still considering Taiwan an economic liability, the emperor nevertheless took these strategic considerations to heart. He wanted no major pirate's lair so near the Chinese southeastern coast, and he was interested in keeping Europeans as far away as possible. Shi Lang's arguments turned the tide in favor of retaining Penghu and Taiwan. In 1684, the 23rd year of Emperor Kangxi's reign, the Qing administration embraced Taiwan and the Penghu island group as territory under its imperial sovereignty. The island that had previously appeared on official maps as rebel-held territory labeled Dongning ("Eastern Peace," the name that Zheng Chenggong had used for Tainan and by extension all territories on the island under his governance) now was designated *Taiwan*.[2]

Shi Lang's arguments concerning Taiwan's strategic value were sound, but the reservations of those who thought that the island would be a continually difficult exercise in governance were also well-founded. Qing officials on Taiwan forever faced difficulties in gaining control over this island frontier at the periphery of the Chinese empire. Qing dynasty efforts to limit expansion of Han Chinese settlement, avoid confrontation with the aborigines, and keep administrative expenses to a minimum represented reasonable but ultimately unattainable objectives that in large measure characterized Qing administrative policy until late in the dynasty's history of governing Taiwan.[3]

QING GOVERNANCE OF TAIWAN

Taiwan and Penghu were placed under the administrative jurisdiction of Fujian province and perceived as similar to nearby Xiamen, another island of Qing and Fujian governance. During Qing rule, provinces usually came under the administrative authority of a governor, typically an ethnic Han Chinese, who reported to a governor-general, commonly an ethnic Manchu who had responsibility for two or three provinces. The governor of Fujian reported to the governor-general of Zhejiang and Fujian, who was thus the top official in the sphere of governance that included Taiwan and Penghu. Taiwan and the islands in the Penghu group were considered a single *fu* (prefecture) under the Fujian provincial administration. The governor of Fujian was actually a rather remote figure in terms of day-to-day administration of Taiwan. The Qing administrative apparatus that more immediately affected the subjects on Taiwan and Penghu operated from the present-day city of Tainan. The prefect with offices there had responsibility for what was then known as Taiwan *fu,* the designation for both the capital and the territories under the prefect's authority on Penghu and Taiwan. Between the prefect of Taiwan *fu* and the governor of Fujian were two other key officials: a circuit intendant who came for a lengthy stay and inspection tour of Taiwan every six months and a coastal defense intendant who was a rival of the prefect and the circuit intendant and who wielded the most military power on the island.[4]

Under the administration of Taiwan *fu* were three *xian* (counties): Taiwan, including the territory immediately surrounding the capital and similar in area to present-day Tainan *xian;* Zhuluo, including the areas for which the *xian* of Taizhong and Jiayi today provide local governance; and Fengshan, essentially today's Gaoxiong *xian.* Still smaller units of governance known as *ting* (subprefectures) were under the authority of the *xian* magistrates. In 1684 the Han Chinese and plains aborigine population totaled only about 130,000. There were in addition some 10,000 army and navy personnel stationed on Taiwan, including a large contingent that patrolled the coast to keep pirates at bay and to prevent Zheng loyalists from returning to challenge Qing occupation of Taiwan.[5]

Internal security was also a chief concern; relations between Han Chinese and the aborigines were an important policy preoccupation at the Qing dynasty court in Beijing. Two views held sway among the emperor's advisers. Some thought the best way to secure the island for Qing authority was to encourage colonization and forceful occupation of aborigine lands for the pursuit of Chinese-style agriculture. Under this approach, the aborigines could be compensated for their territorial losses or could themselves convert to Chinese agricultural practices and assimilate with the Han Chinese population. Indeed, sinicization of the aborigine population in all matters of culture and social organization was the ultimate objective of those who advocated an aggressive colonial policy. The other view stressed the desirability of restricting Han Chinese immigration into Taiwan, keeping to a minimum the territorial infringements on aboriginal hunting grounds and in all ways seeking to reduce the chances for violent confrontations that could cost lives and fiscal resources.[6] This latter view was dominant throughout most of the Qing dynasty's rule of Taiwan. Soon after Qing officials assumed governance of the island, they promulgated three key principles in the court document "Regulations Based on Investigations into the Matter of Emigration to Taiwan" (eventually referred to as "Three Prohibitions with Regard to Refugees"):

1. Those wishing to migrate to Taiwan must apply from their home villages of registration and submit documents for examination by the branch military circuit intendancy for Taiwan and Xiamen; further investigations will be conducted by the Coastal Defense Magistrate's Office. Severe penalties will be invoked in cases of illegal emigration.

2. Those obtaining permission to migrate may not bring family or friends. Those already on Taiwan should not offer encouragement to friends or relatives to apply for emigration from the mainland.

3. Hakka from Chaozhou and Huizhou should not henceforth migrate to Taiwan.[7]

Thus, Taiwan was conceived to be a place where males might work seasonally in agricultural endeavors, then return to the mainland where spouses, children, families, and native villages awaited them. The prohibition on further Hakka immigration was intended to reduce the chance for conflict between that subethnic group, which at the time came mainly from Guangdong province and spoke a different dialect than did the Minnan dialect-speaking majority from Fujian. At the same time, policymakers attempted to ensure that expansion of cultivated lands occurred in a careful and orderly process that respected the rights of the aborigines and their capacity to wreak destruction if aroused. Ample area across the plains was quarantined for the hunting and fishing activities of the aborigines; and the mountains running through the heart of Taiwan, as well as the territory along the rugged east coast, was considered beyond the boundaries of Han Chinese settlement or economic exploitation. Sentries were posted at key passageways to mountain areas, and guards patrolled the boundaries that designated quarantined land. The Qing court promoted a system of taxation of aborigines whereby a local notable collected a per capita tax in kind (usually deer hides) and ensured that the aborigines in their designated areas fulfilled corvee labor obligations. There were 46 such taxpaying units and a like number of notables doing the collecting. Meanwhile, only a limited number of monopoly merchants were licensed to buy hides from the tax farmers. On paper, the plan looked like a logical way to reduce administrative expenses and ensure revenue collections while keeping firm control over Han Chinese interaction with aborigines. In practice, though, the system was ripe for abuse. Temptations were ever present for tax farmers to enrich themselves by collecting imposts above agreed-upon levels. Restive plains aborigines expressed their frustrations with the system by revolting in two different areas during 1699.[8]

Neither were restrictions on immigration practicable. By the early eighteenth century the southeastern coastal areas of mainland China had recovered from years of war and neglect due to the forced removal of people from lands lying 10 *li* (10 to 17 miles) inland from the coast. The farming and fishing economies became productive again, capable of supporting an increase in population. But in a familiar pattern from economic and demographic history, population growth eventually undermined the ability of many people to attain an acceptable livelihood. Residents of the Fujianese areas of Quanzhou and Zhangzhou and the Guangdong areas of Huizhou and Chaozhou were especially hard-pressed. By 1700, more and more land-hungry and desperate people were ignoring the Qing legal proscriptions and braving the Taiwan strait in search of opportunity on the frontier. By 1735, the population on the western plains of Taiwan stood at 415,000 and land under cultivation had grown to 50,517 *jia*. Both figures represented approximately threefold increases since 1684.[9]

Journeys across the turbulent Taiwan strait were always perilous. They became more so when opportunistic ship captains exploited the desperation and naivete of the illegal immigrants. Large ships of the time could transport about 25 people; smaller ships might hold about 17. Men would frequently disguise themselves as sailors, while the elderly, the infirm, and women and children had to hide below the main deck. Those who specialized in arranging the journeys were called *ketou* ("leaders of the guests"), and the straits themselves came to be called the Black Water Ditch for the treacherous waters that claimed so many lives. Shiploads frequently exceeded capacity. The skills of those doing the piloting were often not of high order. Those who signed on as sailors were typically a quarrelsome lot, and melees often broke out over claims on the fees charged to the emigrants on anything of value that the ship might be transporting. The colloquialism *guan shui* ("pouring water") was applied to the unhappy circumstances of a sailor being pushed overboard on the trip to or from Taiwan. Captain and crew of these ships were not above telling hapless immigrants that they had arrived on Taiwan, when actually they were being dumped on some small, forlorn island; this practice was called *fangsheng* (literally, "releasing life"), an expression normally applied to the release of captured animals. Similarly, forcing the migrant to disembark at a still faraway point, struggling to find foothold in sand or mud, came to be known as *zhongyu* ("planting taro"). The act of sitting and watching migrants succumbing to the ocean waves after being cast into the waters became euphemistically known as *siyu* ("feeding the fish"). Under such hardships, the migrants sought help from the goddess Mazu and established numerous temples in her honor. Most famous among these were the Tianhou Gong at Magong, Penghu, and the Chaotian Gong temple at Beigang. Boats gathered in great numbers at the seaside locations of these temples. Migrants offered incense to Mazu, asking her blessing during their continued ventures at sea.[10]

Lyrics of a song sung by those who had experienced the travails of the passage to Taiwan went as follows:

Urge all lords and those you love not to traverse the straits to Taiwan;
Taiwan is suitable as a border post for ghosts;
Cease urging all loved ones from coming to Taiwan,
For the course leading to Taiwan is full of hardship.[11]

Despite this song of warning and the very real dangers it describes, immigration to Taiwan proved steady. For many decades Qing policies did impede the settlement of families in Taiwan and skewed the distribution of population by gender, giving rise to a frontier society populated by foot-loose and frequently unruly single men. Not a few Han Chinese men ultimately sought mates among the aborigines. The power of women in general was enhanced by the gender imbalance. Women enjoyed unusual authority over their husbands under the conditions prevailing in many areas of settlement. The frequency with which women took lovers other than their husbands gave rise to the expression "Taiwanese women possess nine husbands." Although the immigration of Hakka people into Taiwan was formally forbidden for many decades, Hakka men did make their way to Taiwan illegally, thus making the competition for women even more pronounced. As the Hakka and Fujianese immigrants searched for female companionship, those women inclined toward prostitution generally found it to be quite a lucrative trade. Hakka males referred to the Fujianese women to whom they had recourse as "lucky companions"; the women used the euphemism "Hakka elder brothers" in reference to their customers.[12]

Migrants from Guangdong and Fujian continued to defy the official proscriptions against emigration to Taiwan. By the time of the emperor Yongzheng (1722–35), the area south of today's Jiayi, known as Jianan, was well settled. Immigrants from Fujian's Quanzhou and Zhangzhou areas started moving northward to open up new lands for cultivation. Gradually, they made their way up the western coast to Zhanghua, Fengyuan, and Taizhong and were poised to move farther north to Xinzhu, Taibei, and Danshui. Hakka immigrants applied their skills in establishing terraced fields on hillsides and mountain slopes; they settled areas known today by such names as Chisan, Linbian, Donggang, and Fangliao. Han Chinese immigrants also settled areas reaching toward higher elevations midway up the coast along the western plain: Dianfeng, Wufeng, Nantou, Puli, Zhudong, and Beipu. This movement toward the hillsides and mountains brought Han Chinese increasingly into conflict with aborigines, and the population movements in general put great strain on the comparatively few Qing administrative officials on Taiwan, who soon found it difficult to govern the island effectively. In 1721 a major rebellion involving both Fujianese and Hakka immigrants rocked the island. During 1731–32 another violent protest, this time launched by aborigines in the Danshui area, greatly taxed a fledgling administrative framework in northern Taiwan; this disturbance in turn gave heart to Han Chinese rebels in the Fengshan area near today's Gaoxiong.[13]

Under these exigencies of population movements and social unrest, the emperor Yongzheng gave the Qing court official Lan Dingyuan a respectful audience. Lan urged an abandonment of quarantine policies, the aggressive settlement of Taiwan for the purpose of establishing a dynamic agricultural economy, and enough military presence to quell aborigine revolts. Yongzheng found Lan Dingyuan's arguments compelling. Influenced by Lan's views, the emperor authored policies that strengthened the administrative structure on Taiwan and loosened restrictions on immigration. A new county, Zhanghua (which bears the same name today), was created in the same general central area as Zhuluo (today's Jiayi), providing tangible recognition of the population movement northward along the western coast. The highest official there, the Zhanghua *xian* magistrate, had responsibility for northern locations, as well. Within his jurisdiction, a *ting* (one level below the *xian*) was established in Danshui to further extend Qing governmental authority in northern Taiwan. In 1732 immigration restrictions were relaxed, and for the first time families could legally migrate together to Taiwan. During this same period, the Qing government reduced the head tax on the aborigines, placed renewed emphasis on aborigine land claims, and gave official backing to militia consisting of plains aborigines who pledged to defend Qing policies and to Han Chinese settlements against the attacks of mountain-based aboriginal groups.[14]

The more liberal immigration and pro-colonization policy did not last long. The emperor Yongzheng died in 1735, and by the late 1730s Governor-General Hao Youlin was already making administrative decisions with the blessing of the Qing court that once again aimed to slow the pace of immigration. An anti-colonization attitude that lasted throughout the reign

(1736–95) of the Qianlong emperor had become dominant in Beijing, and immigration from the mainland into Taiwan was officially proscribed. Yet, as the shortage of arable land and the population pressure grew more pronounced in Guangdong and Fujian and drove more immigrants across the strait, the anti-colonization effort became a lost cause. By 1735 the chief population area defined by the western plains was already filled with three times the people it had contained in 1684; by 1777, the population along the western coast stood at 839,803—a more than sixfold increase since the beginning of the Qing administration on Taiwan. To adequately govern an increasing and geographically expanding population, the Qing administration by the end of the eighteenth century had put in place four subprefectural units spanning the length of the island: the *ting* administrations for the Penghu islands to the south, the western coastal town of Lugang, the northern port of Danshui, and the northeastern area of Gemalan stretching out from the port city of Jilong. These units had been established in addition to and stood in administrative authority just under the four county-level *(xian)* units of Fengshan, Taiwan, Zhuluo, and Zhanghua.[15]

Typically, population pressures caused the Qing administration to recognize the claims of major landholders and even squatters who had opened up new areas for cultivation. Clinging to the restrictive immigration policy and endeavoring to appease the aborigines, officials would redraw the quarantine boundaries and expend some effort to minimize further expansion into areas claimed by Taiwan's original inhabitants. However effective this might be for certain stretches of time and in given areas of the island, the policy remained a long-term failure. By the 1890s Taiwan's population exceeded 2,500,000 and its area under cultivation exceeded 360,000 *jia;* both figures represented 20-fold increases since 1684. Amid such growth, additional governmental units would inevitably be established to serve key areas of increasing population. During the 1870s the Qing court redesigned the governing structure for the Penghu islands and Taiwan. The dynastic administration established a new Taiwan Circuit that included the prefectures *(fu)* of Taiwan (with headquarters in today's Tainan) and Taibei (centered in today's Danshui, near Taibei). The four *xian* (Fengshan, Taiwan, Jiayi, and Zhanghua) remained the same, but the new *ting* of Puli, Beinan, and Jilong, along with the older *ting* of Lugang and Gemalan, brought the number of these subprefectural units to five. Japanese and French designs on Taiwan greatly heightened the attention of Qing officials to the matter of governing the island. In 1887 a new decree made Taiwan a province consisting of three prefectures: the northern

Taibei *fu,* including the *xian* of Danshui, Xinzhu, and Yilan; the southern Tainan *fu,* including the *xian* of Anping, Jiayi, Fengshan, and Hengchun, as well as Penghu *ting;* and the west-central Taiwan *fu* (the name given at that time not to the Tainan area, as had previously been the case, but rather to the area encompassing today's Taizhong), including the *xian* of Yulin, Miaoli, and Zhanghua, as well as Puli *ting.* Furthermore, the Qing administration now claimed governing responsibility for Taiwan's mountainous and eastern coastal areas. A unit of administration known as *zhou* was established for this area; the central government involved itself in the minutiae of administration at this level, issuing decrees through provincial administrators working at *zhou* headquarters in today's Taidong.[16]

Having embraced responsibility for the governance of Taiwan with some misgivings, Qing administrators by the late nineteenth century were forced by the ineluctable movement of population to add more and more layers to a bureaucratic apparatus that came to encompass the entire island. Only in the 1880s did the dynasty signal that it was ready to establish the kind of formal administration that could truly adequately govern a rather unruly populace on this bustling, brawling frontier. Many of Taiwan's inhabitants had come to the island in contravention of official proscriptions. Han Chinese settlers had demonstrated a will of their own in expanding into lands officially set aside for the residence and economic activities of the aborigines; the latter did not give up their land without a fight: Conflicts between the Chinese and the aborigines were legion. Until the last years of Qing governance of Taiwan, administrators relied heavily on local elites to help local magistrates maintain order. Although the locally powerful did maintain a rough order through a combination of armed force and more peaceable relationships with villagers within their areas of influence, violent confrontations were frequent.[17] The most serious of them, the Zhu Yigui Rebellion of 1721 and the Lin Shuangwen Rebellion of 1787–88, resulted in major administrative adjustments on the part of the Qing court.

REBELLIOUS TAIWAN

In the course of the 212-year Qing rule on Taiwan, large and small rebellions numbered over a hundred, greatly eclipsing the standard embedded in a saying that summarized social unrest in late imperial China: "every three years a small rebellion, every five years a big rebellion." Qing administrators on Taiwan were of mainland provenance, generally natives of areas other than Fujian and Guangdong. Officials at the prefectural and county level were limited to three years of office. They had little natural feel for the areas they presumed to govern, and they had only those ties that they could cultivate quickly and rather artificially. Local magistrates did their best to cultivate such ties with the local elite, people who held significant agricultural property and possessed enough armed force to help keep order. Such locally powerful types could also turn against the representatives of dynastic government if economic conditions or political dissatisfactions seemed to warrant rebellion.[18]

Zhu Yigui was a person of Zhangzhou ancestry who lived in the village of Lohanmen, Fengshan *xian,* in an area today described by the Neimen District of Gaoxiong *xian.*[19] He made a good living raising ducks, and he demonstrated qualities that won the respect and support of much of the local populace. Something of a local Robin Hood, Zhu Yigui acquired a reputation as one who would fight for the rights and come to the assistance of those in need. In 1721, the 60th year of the Kangxi emperor's reign, an earthquake brought great hardship on the people of Zhu Yigui's area of influence. The prefect for Taiwan *fu,* Wang Zhen, also served as the magistrate of Fengshan *xian* but did little to ameliorate the declining fortunes of the people. In fact, he demonstrated a notable lack of empathy by sending his son to collect heavy taxes, impose burdensome fines, and mete out harsh punishments to those who could not pay, even under post-earthquake conditions of damaged fields, low production, and increasing impoverishment. In such circumstances, several hundred people flocked to Zhu Yigui when he raised the standard of rebellion in protest against Wang Zhen's unwise and distinctly non-Confucian disregard for the welfare of the people for whom he had administrative responsibility.[20]

On April 19, 1721, Zhu Yigui's forces attacked and conquered Gangshan, bringing forth a response from a high-ranking military official by the surname of Ouyang. Many of those who answered Ouyang's call to arms were aborigines willing to burn, kill, rape, and plunder Han Chinese communities that had forcefully occupied areas the native inhabitants had originally claimed for their own use. The actions of the aborigines further raised the ire of the Han Chinese and at least temporarily led them to put aside their own subethnic rivalries. An ethnic Hakka named Du Junying rallied to the side of rebellion, leading a force that captured the *xian* seat of Fengshan. Du Junying then joined Zhu Yigui in a combined assault on the administrative capital of Taiwan *fu,* today's Tainan. Qing forces panicked, scattered, and fled virtually without a fight. Civil and military officials fled with their families to Penghu. On May 1, 1721, what was by then considered the Anti-Qing People's Army held Tainan and moved on to take control of Zhuluo (present-day Jiayi). The rebel army moved up the western coastal plains, gaining control of most areas of significant settlement except the northernmost area of Danshui. On May 11, 1721, Zhu Yigui took the title of Reviving King *(zhongxing wang)* in a ceremony at Tainan's Tianhou Temple. He adopted the name Enduring Peace *(yong he)*, ennobling all of his generals and endeavoring to set up a Ming dynasty-style administration.[21]

Before long, though, disorder set in at Zhu Yigui's court. Du Junying, harboring monarchical aspirations for his own family, had sought to install his son as king. Failing, he then took offense at the meager reward extended to him by the new king and his subordinates. There ensued a steady worsening of relations between the Hakka and Fujianese elements in the Anti-Qing People's Army. Soon Zhu Yigui authorized one of his most trusted subordinates to launch an attack on the forces of Du Junying; when the latter suffered a chastening defeat, he retreated northward to Huweixi. Emboldened, Zhu Yigui then sent an even stronger force southward with intent to eliminate any further Hakka threat. It became clear that Zhu had overreached. The threatened Hakka communities organized a determined defense of their homes and villages, now waving banners reading "Great Qing" in a reverse-course show of support for the mainland dynasty of the Manchus. The Hakka forces came away with a decisive victory this time, weakening not only the fighting force but also, at least as important, the prestige of Zhu Yigui.[22]

This turn of events in the Hakka-Fujianese rivalry coincided with an amphibious attack launched by the naval commander for Fujian province, Shi Shipiao, in conjunction with the military commander for the southern seas, Lan Tingzhen. The force landed on June 16, 1721, seizing the old fort at Anping. The landing of the Qing forces dampened enthusiasm for the cause of the rebels, whose specific dissatisfactions and popular support had always been mostly limited to the areas at the extreme southern end of Taiwan. Zhu Yigui did attempt a counterattack but predictably failed miserably. The rebel leader retreated to the Zhuluo (Jiayi) area with a remnant force numbering only about a thousand. Du Junying meanwhile surrendered to the Qing, claiming a rediscovered loyalty to the dynastic government. On June 28, 1721, Qing forces captured Zhu Yigui after villagers of Gou-a-wei betrayed the rebel's position. On February 23, 1722, Zhu and his key subordinates were drawn and quartered.

The representatives of the dynasty proved unsympathetic to Du Junying's change of heart. He and his subordinates were given a quicker execution; they were beheaded a few days after their erstwhile co-rebels had gone to their particularly gruesome deaths. Qing officials now regained primary governing authority, but it took three years to extinguish the rebellion and its offshoots entirely.[23]

An even more consequential and long-lasting rebellion rocked Taiwan in the latter part of the same century. The ancestry of the rebellion's leader, Lin Shuangwen, was traceable to Zhangzhou, the same district in Fujian province from which Zhu Yigui's forebears had migrated to Taiwan.[24] They had settled in a different region of Taiwan, though; and when Lin endeavored to lead his rebellion, he lived in Daliyi village of Zhanghua *xian*. Lin Shuangwen shared with Zhu a capacity for leadership of impoverished people. In Lin's case, heading a branch of the Heaven and Earth Society gave him ample opportunity to share society members' concerns and articulate programs for action. In 1786, the 51st year of the Qianlong emperor's reign, Qing officials searched and arrested a group of Lin Shuangwen's fellow Heaven and Earth Society members in an attempt to forestall any rebellious activity stemming from their "Oppose the Qing; Restore the Ming" credo. The dynastic officials proceeded to rough up members of the local populace without making a distinction between those maintaining Heaven and Earth membership or even the propensity to rebel, on the one hand, and those simply going about their everyday pursuits, on the other. There is no doubt, though, that the local populace entertained no overwhelming fondness for the Qing representatives who brought them what they knew of official governance: On January 16, 1787, stirred into action by the coarse and unwarranted actions of the officials, those who shared Lin Shuangwen's antipathy to the dynastic authorities helped launch the best-organized, largest-scale, longest rebellion in Taiwanese history.[25]

The rebels quickly seized the areas known today as Taizhong, Zhanghua, and Xinzhu. Lin Shuangwen felt emboldened to assume the monarchical title of King of the Ming *(ming wang)*, with the reign name of Shuntian. He established his offices temporarily in Zhanghua. After taking nearby Zhuluo, the rebels moved southward through the heart of the productive western plains, advancing all the way to Tainan. Soldiers were stationed in strategic locations along this route, encompassing a significant territorial expanse from southern into what was then regarded as northern Taiwan. To the south, Heaven and Earth leader Zhuang Datian brought Fengshan *xian* under control. But in three great battles in which the rebels attacked from both sea and land, anti-Qing forces led by Lin Shuangwen and Zhuang Datian failed to gain control of the prefectural capital at Tainan. The Qing rushed in reinforcements, regrouped, and made a successful effort to regain Zhuluo. Lin Shuangwen then gathered 100,000 supporters unto his army for a sustained siege of that county seat, but five months of fierce battle found the dynastic forces to have sufficient staying power to hold Zhuluo. Then help for the Qing loyalists arrived in the person of Fu Kangan, fresh from a frontier post as Shaanxi-Gansu governor-general. Fu led 100,000 crack troops ashore at Lugang and proceeded without delay toward Zhuluo. After one day of extremely hard fighting, the rebels lifted their siege and withdrew from their positions surrounding the city.[26]

Subethnic rivalry came to undermine the forces of Lin Shuangwen in much the same way as such tensions had undercut the Zhu Yigui rebellion. Lin Cou, a person of Quanzhou heritage, exploited the unsettled conditions on the western plains to launch an attack on traditional nemeses from Zhangzhou. The Quanzhou forces threw their support to Qing officialdom and in this role helped the dynastic forces recover Zhanghua and Xinzhu. These forces of Quanzhou subethnicity then joined the regular *ting* forces in pursuit of the rebels, who now faced defeat after defeat. Lin Shuangwen retreated, made a stand at Dali, and experienced another defeat before heading for the mountains in search of safe haven. Once again, a familiar motif described his fate: An area resident betrayed his position, which led to his capture February 10, 1788. He was executed along with his parents, wife, and a number of followers, most of whom had confessed to their rebellious deeds. Their admissions elicited no mercy from officials, who executed 33 of Lin Shuangwen's supporters in all.[27]

TAIWANESE ECONOMIC DEVELOPMENT DURING QING RULE

After the Qing dynasty assumed control of Taiwan in 1683, the system of land tenure was simplified and in general the level of taxation was made less onerous. Land that had previously been held by the Zheng government, reserved for cultivation by self-sustaining military camps, or managed by private individuals favored by the Zheng family became entirely privatized. Now all land was officially considered *mintian* (the people's lands), though in reality most land was not owned by the humble folk who did the actual cultivation. Through the late seventeenth century, when settlement of Taiwan still overwhelmingly encompassed the southern part of the island, most land was controlled by those wealthy enough to sponsor people for migration to Taiwan and provide them with the agricultural implements, draft animals, seeds, and water-conservancy technology necessary to get a sustaining yield from the land. The desire to own the land one cultivated was a major reason for the push northward and even eastward, toward mountain slopes, during the eighteenth century. Eventually much of this land, too, came under landlord control. In part this control came in the form of patents granted for land reclamation by the Qing government, once government officials acknowledged that settlement in a given area had become a reality. In such situations, the regime understood that some accommodation of Han Chinese and aboriginal interests had to be struck. The first to receive official permission to open up new lands for agricultural development were those with the wherewithal to develop the land most economically and to pay regular compensation to aborigines for lands that they lost in the reclamation process. And even when humbler folk struck out to reclaim land for their own agricultural pursuits, the costs of cultivation over time frequently caused these farmers to succumb to pressure, giving up their land to wealthier folk and accepting a tenancy relationship.[28]

Whatever private interest owned the land, fields were classified into upper, middle, and lower grades for both wetfield and nonirrigated types, resulting in a classification scheme of six grades. Wetfield was taxed at about twice the rate of comparable-grade nonirrigated land; the lowest grade of wetfield was usually taxed at about the same rate as the highest grade of nonirrigated fields. Private landholders, frequently landlords who did not work the land themselves, were responsible for tax payments. During the 1683–1777 period, private landholders paid a tax rate of about 13.5 percent of the yield on lower-grade wetfield and 15.7 percent on upper-grade wetfield. Landlords typically passed on this tax burden to tenants and collected an additional 15 percent of the land's yield, resulting in a 30 percent rental rate for farmers. Rents of course varied considerably from region to region, rising to as high as 50 percent of the annual yield or even higher in some areas. When they got this high, the ordinary peasant lived on the bare margins of economic survival. If, under such slim margin of error, natural disasters in the form of earthquakes, floods, or typhoons hit Taiwan, people might very well turn desperate and the ever-present possibility of rebellion on this island frontier could become reality.[29]

Rents could be high in given locations, but in general tax rates prevailing in Taiwan during Qing governance were moderate. A series of tax revisions during 1727–31 caused rates to fall below already moderate levels. An adjustment in 1744 led to slightly higher rates again, but these remained at approximately 15 percent of the annual yield throughout the years of Qing rule. During 1842–43 efforts were made by local magistrates to force a move toward collection in Spanish bullion, by then a currency of wide use in Asian-Pacific trade. Protests from powerful landed interests stifled this effort, though, and tax collections were mainly made in kind.

Administrative limits of the premodern era and a certain leniency on the part of Qing emperors regarding taxation on the island frontier meant that much land went untaxed. As of 1790 untaxed cultivated lands probably reached 3,730 *jia* or more. A century later, Governor Liu Mingchuan's 1890 survey of Taiwan's resources revealed that 220,110 *jia*—about 75 percent of the total 290,000 *jia* under cultivation—were going untaxed. Liu brought much of this land under government taxation, but his survey had not accurately located and recorded even half of the land under cultivation. Just prior to Japanese assumption of power on Taiwan in 1895, 53.5 percent of all land actually under cultivation was not bearing a tax burden.[30]

Mercantile life thrived in the towns that grew up along the coast and those inland settlements of urban character serving the marketing needs of Taiwan's farmers. In late 1684, soon after Taiwan was entered on the official map of the Qing dynasty, the government removed restrictions on all goods traded to the island except saltpeter and military hardware. Ships based in Jiangsu, Zhejiang, Fujian, and Guangdong traded with merchants from Holland, Japan, Manila, and Luzon. Records from 1697 indicate that Taiwanese sugar was especially sought for trade and that rice and other grains, hemp, beans, deerskins, and venison were also valued Taiwanese exports. Japan and Luzon were especially eager markets for Taiwanese sugar. Increased immigration to Taiwan led to rising demand for a number of consumer items from the mainland, and in the early eighteenth century a lively trade transpired: Taiwanese rice and sugar went to mainland China in exchange for needles and thread, dry goods, umbrellas, bricks, liquor, pots, and beans.[31]

An account of 1722 indicates that Taiwanese agricultural goods and game were by that time being incorporated into an intricate trade network prevailing on the mainland. Ships representing merchants from Zhangzhou sailed to Taiwan carrying silk thread, gauze, cut felt, paper materials, tobacco, cloth, straw mats, bricks, gongs, umbrellas, oranges, pomelos, tangerines, cakes, and dried persimmons. These returned from Taiwan with rice, wheat, sugar, beans, potatoes, venison, camphor, taro, hemp, leeks, and fish fins. These items were traded for, or combined with, cargo from such places as Quanzhou, Xinghua, and Fuzhou and shipped to ports along China's eastern coast, particularly Shanghai and Ningbo. From there goods of Taiwan origin made their way inland to places such as Suzhou and northward all the way to Manchuria. In Taiwan, merchant associations specializing in goods destined for the mainland were founded, the first in the port of Luermen in the Tainan area in 1740, followed by others in places such as Xingang, Lugang, and Fengshan sometime after 1768.[32]

In the aftermath of the Opium Wars (1839–42) and the confrontation with the British and French (1859–60), Danshui was among 16 Chinese ports opened to trade. Soon, European traders were ever more present at Jilong, Gaoxiong, Lugang, and Anping too. In 1862 the British trading firm of Jardine, Matheson, and Company formally opened operations in Taiwan; a year later the Qing administration established customs stations off Taiwan, then in 1864 founded permanent stations in the ports of Gaoxiong and Anping. With these events Taiwan became an increasingly important center of European trade with China; foreign interest in the island also caused Qing officials to give greater priority to governing Taiwan.[33]

Between 1868 and 1894 the growth of trade from Taiwanese ports was greater than China's trade growth as a whole. An unfavorable balance of trade for Taiwan in the 1860s and early 1870s soon shifted so that by 1874 the island registered favorable trade balances. Of goods imported from foreign countries, the most important were opium, cotton finished goods, woolens, and metals. By the 1882–91 period, values attached to certain imports flowing through the ports of South Taiwan yielded the following percentages: opium, 78.5 percent; cotton, 7.1 percent; woolens, 5.3 percent; metals, 0.3 percent; and miscellaneous items, 8.8 percent. Through the southern ports of Gaoxiong and Tainan came opium, scrap iron, nails, clubs, lead for the manufacture of tea boxes, kerosene, flour, matches, cuttlefish, and dried shrimp. Through the northern port of Danshui came Japanese cotton cloth and Indian cotton yarn, woolen accessory items, and bags for manufactured tea. Japanese and Taiwanese merchants were developing a close trade relationship during these years; imports of matches into Taiwan came entirely from Japan and increased 6.2 times in volume from 1882 to 1891.[34]

Until about 1860 northern Taiwan produced enough rice to feed people in that part of the island and to export a portion of the yield, as well. Thereafter, an increasing urban population created a demand in the North that could not be met by farmers in the region or by supplements from the South. Hence, after 1860 northern Taiwan imported rice from the mainland. Records indicate that Taiwan imported 3,951 tons of mainland rice in 1882; that figure rose to 5,425 tons in 1891. Other imports from the mainland included bricks, incense, paper, umbrellas, noodles, pork, peanut oil, tobacco, alum, earthenware, and porcelain. Yet, by the 1868–1894 period the total import value from foreign countries was five times the value of imports from mainland China (although if opium were excluded from the tallies, the value of foreign imports would have been only 1.6 times greater than mainland import values).[35]

Of exports from Taiwan during the 1868–94 period, tea (53.8 percent) and sugar (36.2 percent) comprised fully 90 percent of the total. Exports increased more than eightfold over the 27-year period. Tea exports were mainly of the oolong variety, which had been introduced from Amoy in 1866 by a Briton named John Dodd. Dodd lent farmers capital for cultivating tea and took a heavy profit himself through international trade. By 1870 tea cultivation had reached 630.8 tons, and demand was great enough to accommodate the doubling of prices paid to farmers. In 1870 Robert H. Bruce established Tait and Company for the export of tea, and by 1872 several foreign tea-exporting firms operating from northern Taiwan sent 1,167.6 tons to foreign markets. A report from one major tea-growing region of northern Taiwan in 1877 found all hillsides covered with tea.[36] With product supplied mainly by cultivation on these northern hills, tea exports reached 5,428.3 tons in 1880 and 8,651.2 tons in 1893.

In addition to tea export firms, 150 firms involved in manufacturing tea existed by the year 1900, employing between 100 and 300 women per firm during the busy months and up to 400 or 500 if a big crop demanded extra labor. Thus, in a peak year, as many as 75,000 workers might be employed in tea-manufacturing factories; the yearly average in the major tea-growing areas of the North was 20,000 workers. Profits for the manufacturing and exporting firms were high, stimulating a steady and rapid growth of tea exports from the island. Most of the tonnage (84.8 percent) went to U.S. markets by the 1892–94 period, with European markets taking the largest share of the rest (5.9 percent of the total). These markets overwhelmingly preferred oolong, although the paochung variety introduced in 1881 by Wu Fuyuan from the mainland found a small market niche. Paochung tea mostly passed through Amoy and Hong Kong to Java and the Straits colonies; the remainder went to Swatow, Saigon, Hawaii, and San Francisco. Taiwanese tea farmers profited greatly by tapping into the export market. Prices rose 2.5-fold between 1868 and 1894 and were high enough above production costs to yield a profit of 97.5 percent in 1880 and a still-robust 78 percent in 1881.[37]

Sugar exports enjoyed a similar increase, from 9,581 tons in 1856 to 44,024 tons in 1894, although the growth pattern showed greater fluctuation than tea and actually peaked in 1880 at 58,510 tons. Most sugar production took place in the South, specifically in the Tainan region, which produced 82 percent of the total. The port of Gaoxiong exported 99.5 percent of the sugar destined for foreign markets, whereas the remaining 0.5 percent passed through Danshui. Sugar exports to China went primarily to Zhefu, Tianjin, Shanghai, and Ningbo. Japan took most of the foreign-export share (98.2 percent in 1890–94); Australia was the next-largest foreign market. Foreign markets generally accounted for more than 60 percent of total sugar export tonnage during the 1875–89 period, but from 1890 to 1894 exports to the Chinese mainland (52 percent) slightly exceeded exports to foreign markets (48 percent).[38]

The period of Qing rule was enormously eventful for Taiwanese history, economy, and agriculture. Certain themes introduced into the history of the Taiwanese people would endure into Japanese and Guomindang periods of control on the island. Taiwan's contemporary economic success would be based on the efforts of a populace given to hard work and the pursuit of material gain as a religious imperative. It would be founded on a rice- and sugar-based economy and the responsiveness of Taiwanese farmers and merchants to the opportunities offered by international trade. All of these elements were present in the Taiwanese agrarian-based economy and society that had evolved by the late nineteenth century. The Japanese period that succeeded Qing governance of Taiwan reinforced most of the trends that had been present in Taiwanese history and added elements of authoritarian rule and rapid technological progress that would also greatly inform the contemporary Taiwanese experience.

THE IMPACT OF WESTERN AND JAPANESE IMPERIALISM

During the Opium Wars, the Qing administration closely guarded Taiwan. In 1841 an English fleet sailed into Jilong, opening fire on the Sanshawan battery emplacement and executing the first attack of the Qing era by foreigners. The Qing battery guard returned fire, breaking the mast rope of the British ship; further, as the British ship retreated, it ran into a reef and sank. From this time forward, the government on Taiwan adopted a repel-the-barbarian, closed-door policy.[39]

In 1871, as 69 mariners from the Ryukyus were on their way to China to offer tribute, they were blown off course and landed on Taiwan at a spot in today's Manzhou *xiang* (township) in Pingdong *xian*. Aborigines from Mudan village killed 54 of the sailors. At the time, Ryukyu people recognized both China and Japan as their sovereign states. Japan sent a remonstration to the Chinese over the incident, but the Qing court claimed that the Ryukyu shipmates had landed on an area of aboriginal settlement not within the administrative domain of the Chinese empire. Thus conceding that it did not govern the entire island of Taiwan, the Qing court disclaimed responsibility for the actions of the aborigines in Mudan. Japan had long coveted Taiwan, so in 1874 it took this opportunity to establish a so-called Taiwan Aborigine Affairs Office at Zhang Ji in Pingdong *xian*. To this end, the Japanese sent an armed force ashore at Sheliao in Pingdong, where it met stiff resistance from aborigine folk. The chief of Mudan village died in battle and the entire settlement was torched, inducing all other settlements to surrender. The Japanese army established a fort and various other houses and buildings in the area and settled in for long-term residence. The Qing government then recognized the gravity of the situation and invested Shen Baozhen with the duty of managing Taiwan's defenses; Shen also entered into talks with the Japanese, in the end yielding an agreement mediated by the British. The Qing administration agreed to pay military reparations, to compensate the Japanese for expenditures on roads and buildings, and to provide a sizable monetary allotment for general relief. The dynasty also accepted administrative authority in the area and agreed to take responsibility for the behavior of the aborigines residing in that part of Taiwan.[40]

Shen Baozhen was one of three highly placed Qing officials who helped make Taiwan the most technologically advanced area within the Chinese empire. This startling technological development at the fringes of Qing governance was stimulated by the interest that Westerners and Japanese were showing in this strategically located island and associated smaller islands. Shen was director of the Fuzhou naval yard when in 1874 he was made an imperial commissioner with special administrative authority on Taiwan. In his high administrative post in Fujian, he had already begun to take an interest in Taiwan, which then was still administratively part of Fujian. During the years 1867–75, Shen promoted Western-style coal extraction operation methods in the mines near Jilong. He began an aggressive pacification and sinicization program aimed at transforming economic, cultural, and social orientations of aborigines. From 1874 to 1875 Shen Baozhen superintended the construction of 859 *li* (307.5 miles) of additional roads stretching into the mountainous areas at northern, central, and southern points plotted so as to exert the Qing presence in aboriginal areas throughout the island. Shen also oversaw the establishment of a number of new-style schools *(yixue)* that emphasized Western math, science, and approaches to a variety of disciplines over the traditional schools' heavy literary bias and focus on passing the civil service exam. Shen also advocated the laying of a cable for telegraphic linkage between Amoy and Taiwan.[41]

Ding Richang, in his capacity of Fujian governor, became the second great modernizer on Taiwan. From late 1875 through mid-1878 his policies were dominant on the island. Following the lead of Shen Baozhen, his government in 1877 issued 21 regulations detailing cultural and economic assimilation policies meant to bring aborigine beliefs and institutions into greater consonance with those of the Han Chinese. At about the same time, Ding was hatching a plan for a north-south railroad to run the entire length of Taiwan; this scheme was mere fantasy, though, for neither the technological expertise nor the financial commitment necessary for such an undertaking was in evidence on the island at that time.[42]

After Ding Richang's tenure as governor of Fujian ended in 1878, a six-year period passed in which administrative energy in the governance of Taiwan diminished. Then the most remarkable of the three modernizers made his appearance on the island in July 1884. Liu Mingchuan came to the governorship of Fujian with a long record of distinguished service in behalf of the dynasty. Liu's attentions on Taiwan were first drawn to the immediate crisis of the Sino-French War (1884–85). When the French sent a fleet to bombard Jilong, he authorized a fierce reply from the Qing army. Soon the French, reeling from defeat on both land and sea, retreated to ships that for a time kept a safe distance offshore. The forces overseen by Liu Mingchuan managed to seal off the port at Jilong for two months before the French army staged a comeback, inducing the flight of Liu Mingchuan to Danshui. Jilong fell, and the French army and naval forces pressed the attack to Danshui. But the French forces sustained numerous casualties, and in time tropical diseases ravaged the French soldiers. Ultimately, the attackers had to retreat. In the aftermath, the island was again returned to sealed-off status. The next year the French army launched another successful attack on Jilong. Qing forces met defeat after defeat, but they were tenacious enough that the French government decided not to press the attack further. In a mixed response to the government's counsel for peace, the French forces evacuated Taiwan but shelled sections of Penghu as they came to that island chain. When the general hostilities between China and France ceased in 1885, the French army at last disavowed further designs on Jilong and Penghu.[43]

Soon after the Sino-French conflict came to a conclusion, the Qing court made the momentous decision to make Taiwan a province of China, separating its governance from that of Fujian and elevating Taiwan's administrative status from prefecture level to province. In 1887, Liu Mingchuan officially assumed the position of governor of Taiwan province while concurrently holding the post of governor of Fujian. However, the governor-general of Fujian and Zhejiang assumed direct administrative responsibility for Fujian, in practical terms freeing Liu to focus his considerable energies on governance of Taiwan.[44]

In 1885 Liu removed his rival Liu Ao from his duty in southern Taiwan and further undercut those in the southern power center of the island by moving the capital. While construction of a new capital began in the area of today's Taizhong, Liu and his staff occupied Taibei, with the thought that the city would be just a temporary capital. Liu's bold move polarized the island's political actors along regional lines, but it also signaled that a new day had come to the governance of Taiwan. Liu's programs and policies were consistent with the signal. In one of his first and most important actions, Liu ordered that an extensive survey be conducted to determine the amount of land under cultivation and the prevailing patterns of land tenure. Although Liu was not successful in bringing all cultivated land onto official government registers, his survey resulted in the clearest information available regarding the land and patterns of ownership and tenancy.[45]

Through the survey, Liu Mingchuan found that a land tenure system including at least two levels of ownership typically prevailed for each tract of land. One level of ownership lay with the original purchaser of the land, who in many cases had been long absent from the area. The second level of ownership lay with a person who had been subcontracted to provide agricultural management and who bore tax-collecting responsibility. This second landowning type, known as the small-rent *(xiaozu)* owner, in time replaced the original purchaser, known as the big-rent *(dazu)* owner, as the real power in the countryside. Liu's government reduced by 40 percent the amount of annual yield that *xiaozu* holders had to remit to *dazu* holders. Recognizing that the *xiaozu* claimants were those truly in contact with cultivators and with local circumstances, Liu sought to elevate their position in the land tenure system and to begin a process of simplifying the landholding structure. In the meantime, the survey had the immediate effect of bringing more land onto the tax rolls, increasing the revenue from land and poll taxes nearly threefold.[46]

Yet the provincial administration of Liu Mingchuan was not dependent on the land and population-based taxes. These in fact together constituted only the third-largest source of provincial revenue and represented only 11.7 percent of the total. Maritime (22.6 percent) and transit (15.1 percent) were the largest sources, while income from government-owned coal mines, steamships, and railways yielded another 18.2 percent. In addition, the new provincial administration on Taiwan received an annual subsidy from the Fujian provincial treasury that amounted to 10 percent of total revenues, an indication of the Qing administration's support of Taiwan's modernization. This financial largesse was invested in numerous programs of technological innovation. Under Liu Mingchuan's tenure as governor, electric lighting came to Taibei and other important economic and political centers. Modern machinery was used in the lumber, coal-mining, sugar-refining, and brick-making industries. Factories produced modern cannon and rifles, and well-stocked arsenals featuring these armaments signaled an elevated military capability. Telegraphic service connected the Taiwanese cities of Danshui, Jilong, and Tainan; further, a cable laid across the Taiwan strait brought telegraphic communication between Danshui and Fuzhou, the capital of Fujian province. The provincial administration ran a steamship line with six modern vessels and established the humble beginnings of railway service: During Liu Mingchuan's term as governor of Taiwan, rail service began from Jilong to Taibei. Workers on the project already under way proceeded during the early months of Liu Mingchuan's successor's administration to lay rail further southward to Xinzhu.[47]

Liu Mingchuan also continued an irreversible trend, begun under imperial commissioner Shen Baozhen during 1867–75, to sinicize the aborigines and bring them more fully under government control. The headquarters of a bureau created to coordinate the aborigine sinicization program was established south of Taibei, and a second major outpost of the bureau was established about halfway down the eastern coast. Eight local bureaus with 18 branch offices served as tangible evidence of the government's resolve in the matter of aborigine pacification. The efforts of the staff implementing the provincial policy brought new sources of education, sanitation, and transportation to the island's original inhabitants, but they also brought what many aborigines saw as unwarranted and unwanted interference in their traditions and way of life. During Liu Mingchuan's 1884–91 stay on Taiwan, he was forced to commit significant resources and manpower in numerous campaigns to quell aborigine rebellions, especially among the Atayal and the Ami of the northern mountains. One-third of the Qing soldiers killed on Taiwan during this period died in these campaigns against aborigine rebels. Neither did the tradition of Han Chinese rebellion end during Liu Mingchuan's period as governor. Soldiers doing the bidding of the government had to fight tenaciously to bring order to a vast area stretching from Zhanghua to Fengshan in 1888.[48]

Perhaps Liu Mingchuan attempted too much, too soon. Rebels among the aborigines were not his only opponents. His rather swift policy implementation and heavy-handed methods were often at odds with locally powerful elements. Rural taxpayers and remitters of rent in many places throughout the island were forced to yield up more than ever in outlays that directly or indirectly went to the government.. Many of those with interests in the mercantile economy were hit harder, too, with dues on exports, imports, and goods in transit that represented significant sources of government revenue. Liu Mingchuan was the single most impressive individual to take the reins of leadership on Taiwan, and he made Taiwan the most advanced showcase of modernization among the lands claimed by the Qing. But he also brought forceful complaint from many directions. His term of office had not quite expired when he was recalled in 1891. His successor, Shou Youlian, allowed certain projects, such as railway construction as far as Xinzhu, to move toward completion, but for the most part the new governor-general began a retrenchment that affected much of Liu Mingchuan's modernization program. Numerous bureaus were dismantled, construction on the proposed new capital at Taizhong ended, and even the railway project was terminated after the rail to Xinzhu had been laid.[49]

Ambitious modernization would not proceed until at least another five years had passed. By that time it was not the Chinese dynasty of the Qing that controlled Taiwan but rather a newly arrived colonial regime answering to the remarkable modernizers of Meiji Japan.

NOTES

1. Zhou Mingfeng, *Taiwan jian shi* [A concise history of Taiwan] (Taibei: Qian Wei Press, 1994), p. 42.

2. Zhou Mingfeng, pp. 42–43; Qi Jialin, *Taiwan shi* [The history of Taiwan], vol. 1 (Taibei: Sanmin Book Company), p. 139.

3. John Robert Shepherd, in *Statecraft and Political Economy on the Taiwan Frontier* (Stanford, Calif.: Stanford University Press, 1993), on p. 106 discusses the arguments of Shi Lang; the theme of Qing policy with regard to the aborigines is among those that dominate the book. He gives a good overview of the book's themes on pp. 14–21. See also Qi Jialin, pp. 31–41 and 180–94.

4. Zhou Mingfeng, p. 32; Qi Jialin, vol. 2, pp. 16–20.

5. Zhou Mingfeng, p. 33.

6. Shepherd, *Statecraft,* pp. 15–18 and 182–91. Also see Shepherd's article, "The Island Frontier of the Qing," in Murray A. Rubinstein, ed., *Taiwan: A New*

History (Armonk, N.Y.: M. E. Sharpe, 1999), pp. 107–32, especially pp. 108–9, 112–13, and 115–16. Qi Jialin, pp. 31–41, also covers matters of Qing policy relevant to Han Chinese migration and Han Chinese–aborigine interaction on the Taiwan frontier.

7. Zhou Mingfeng, p. 47. The Hakka people, originally from northern China, had by the seventeenth century migrated southward, settling mainly in Guangdong province. Their dialect was different from the Minnan dialect that was dominant in Fujian.

8. Ibid., pp. 52–53; Qi Jialin, pp. 31–41. A *jia* is roughly equal to a hectare, or about 2.5 acres.

9. Zhou Mingfeng, pp. 49–50; Qi Jialin, pp. 197 and 204.

10. Zhou Mingfeng, pp. 47–48.

11. Ibid., p. 48.

12. Ibid.

13. Ibid., pp. 49–50.

14. Shepherd, in *Statecraft,* pp. 15–16, raises issues addressed during the Yongzheng era, and on pp. 185–90 he gives considerable attention to the ideas of Lan Dingyuan. See also pp. 115–16 of his article in Rubinstein.

15. Zhou Mingfeng, pp. 52–53. Qi Jialin has a concise, very informative summary of Han Chinese settlement in southern Taiwan (p. 198), through the central regions (pp. 199–200), and across the northern part of the island to the eastern seaboard (pp. 201–4).

16. Zhou Mingfeng, pp. 48–50.

17. Zhou Mingfeng, p. 54; Qi Jialin, p. 179.

18. Ibid.

19. Zhou Mingfeng, p. 55.

20. Ibid.; Huang Dashou, pp. 138–39.

21. Zhou Mingfeng, p. 55; Huang Dashou, *Taiwan shi gang* [An outline history of Taiwan] (Taibei, Sanmin Book Company, 1982), pp. 139–41.

22. Zhou Mingfeng, p. 55; Huang Dashou, pp. 142–43.

23. Zhou Mingfeng, p. 56; Huang Dashou, pp. 145–46.

24. Zhou Mingfeng, pp. 56–57; Huang Dashou, pp. 146–47.

25. Ibid.

26. Zhou Mingfeng, p. 57; Huang Dashou, p. 147.

27. Zhou Mingfeng, p. 57; Huang Dashou, pp. 147–48. Qi Jialin, pp. 187–94, discusses the ultimate effectiveness of Qing policy in dealing with serious outbreaks of popular discontent.

28. Qi Jialin, p. 205; Wu Congxian, *Zhongguo nongye fazhan* [Chinese agricultural development] (Taibei: Central Research Documents Agency, 1984), pp. 507–12.

29. Qi Jialin, pp. 206–8; Wu Congxian, p. 510.

30. Qi Jialin, p. 210; Wu Congxian, p. 510.

31. Qi Jialin, p. 215.

32. Qi Jialin, pp. 215–17; Zhou Mingfeng, p. 50.

33. Qi Jialin, pp. 219–20; Zhou Mingfeng, p. 51.

34. Qi Jialin, pp. 221–24; Zhou Mingfeng, pp. 51–52.

35. Zhou Mingfeng, p. 51; Qi Jialin, p. 221.

36. Qi Jialin, pp. 226–28; Zhou Mingfeng, pp. 51–52.

37. Qi Jialin, pp. 227–30; Zhou Mingfeng, pp. 51–52.

38. Qi Jialin, pp. 228–30; Zhou Mingfeng, p. 51.

39. Zhou Mingfeng, p. 58; Huang Dashou, pp. 181–84.

40. Zhou Mingfeng, pp. 58–59; Huang Dashou, pp. 184–88.

41. Robert Gardella, "From Treaty Ports to Provincial Status, 1860–1894," in Rubinstein, pp. 184–85. Qi Jialin, pp. 57–72, and Huang Dashou, pp. 154–60, also have good discussions of the contributions of Shen Baozhen to the development of Taiwan in the late Qing era.

42. Gardella, pp. 185–86. Good discussions of the contributions of Ding Richang are also found on pp. 73–84 in Qi Jialin and pp. 160–64 in Huang Dashou.

43. Zhou Mingfeng, p. 59. On the impact of the Sino-French War on late Qing Taiwan, see Qi Jialin, pp. 85–97 and 99–114, and Huang Dashou, pp. 188–92.

44. Zhou Mingfeng, pp. 61–62; Huang Dashou, pp. 165–70. For a fine summary of Ziu Mingchuan's tenure on Taiwan, see also Gardella, pp. 187–94.

45. Qi Jialin, pp. 115–20.

46. Huang Dashou, pp. 171–73.

47. Qi Jialin, pp. 125–38; Huang Dashou, pp. 173–75.

48. Qi Jialin, pp. 121–24.

49. Ibid., pp. 138–45; Huang Dashou, p. 180.

Chapter 5

JAPANESE COLONIAL RULE, 1895–1945

Factional squabbling at the Korean court in Seoul precipitated a war between China and Japan that greatly altered the course of Taiwanese history. Korea, with its peninsular thrust toward the islands of Japan and its strategic location to the east of Manchuria, had long been an area in which the Chinese and the Japanese competed for influence. When in 1894 contending factions at the Korean court each sought some decisive contingent of support that could tip the balance in its favor, one faction turned to China, the other to Japan. This gave each of the major powers of East Asia—one an old, venerable titan of civilization having difficulty adjusting to the realities of a European-led modernity, the other in the midst of one of the swiftest, most remarkable politico-economic transformations in history—an opportunity to gain dominance on the strategic Korean peninsula. The Qing court entered into this conflict with all of the hubris that a 3,500-year history of cultural domination in East Asia had understandably inculcated; the Qing court, still operating in a traditional mindset with regard to international relations, endeavored to teach the Japanese upstarts who was still the chief power of East Asia. The Japanese Meiji administration for its part entered into the conflict with the entirely modern mindset of a budding imperial power desiring colonial possessions, meaning prestige and greater economic power in the world that the European industrial revolution had wrought. To the surprise of the Chinese, much of the international community, and even a good number of well-informed Japanese, Japan won the 1894–95 Sino-

Japanese War. The histories of East Asia and Taiwan had taken a dramatic turn.[1]

Seeking peace, the Chinese met with the Japanese at Shimonoseki. Japan was able to secure the promise of a substantial indemnity, but more importantly its representatives sought key territorial acquisitions. According to the terms of the Treaty of Shimonoseki, signed on April 17, 1895, and given final Qing central government approval on May 8, 1895, the Liaodong peninsula of Manchuria passed to Meiji control, as did the Penghu islands and Taiwan. Soon, the governments of Russia, Germany, and France exerted pressure on the Japanese to relinquish Liaodong, which thus reverted to formal Qing control. Yet, this area had been just one of several major points in the region where the real competition was between Russia and Japan for spheres of influence. The Qing court hoped that the international community would also strongly object to Japan's acquisition of Taiwan, at least turning the island into a joint mandate governed by a consortium of interested powers. But the stakes in Taiwan were not high enough for either the Chinese or Western powers to pressure the Japanese government to relinquish Taiwan. Ultimately, the Qing court gave up Taiwan with no notable show of regret.[2]

Resistance as much as regret, though, invested the spirit of those on Taiwan who did object to the prospect of Japanese rule. On May 25, 1895, less than two weeks after the Chinese imperial court had approved the Treaty of Shimonoseki, Qing official Tang Jingsong declared himself the president of a new Republic of Taiwan. As an indication of the political immaturity and confused identity among those in positions of leadership on Taiwan, this would-be president gave a reign title for his putative republic that was entirely consonant with the imperial tradition of China: His reign was to bear the title *Yongqing,* meaning "forever Qing." The declared republic was to have a flag featuring a yellow tiger on a field of blue, with characters bearing the message "president of Taiwan." The flag flew at ceremonies in Taibei, complete with cannon salute, various proclamations in support of the republic's founding, and the announcement of a number of administrative decrees. The fledgling president recognized another Qing official, Qiu Fengjia, as vice president and gave him the practical responsibility for troops that were to encircle and hold Taizhong. Liu Yongfu, the leader of an important militia group known as the Black Flag troops, was installed as head of the republic's army and given the major responsibility of guarding Tainan, where Liu and his Black Flag units were truly powerful. Another official named Chen Jitong assumed the office of foreign affairs chief. Plans for an assembly composed of all major gentry elements on the island were announced. But the proposed leader of the assembly immediately set a precedent that other leaders of the resistance would eventually follow. Chen fled to the mainland, and the assembly never met.[3]

On May 29, 1895, Japanese imperial guards landed on Taiwan just south of Jilong, the first Japanese to arrive since the island had been signed over to the colonial regime. Braves recruited to fight on behalf of the new republic scattered as the Japanese forces made their landing. On June 3 a combined naval and army force attacked Jilong and Shiquiling, again getting the best of Taiwanese forces of resistance. The defeated Taiwanese braves fled to Taibei, where they transformed themselves into bandits, burning, killing, raping, and robbing according to inclination, turning what was supposed to be a show of resistance against colonial masters into personal aggrandizement at the expense of those in the capital city. Tang Jingsong had by this time sent his mother to a secluded spot at the island's interior. With Taibei in turmoil and the Japanese approaching, Tang slipped out of the city at dusk on June 4 and into a foreign business firm located in Danshui. On the evening of June 6 Tang boarded a British ship bound for Xiamen. A number of civil and military officials as well as businesspeople were drawing the same conclusions as Tang with regard to the inevitability of Japanese rule and the futility of resistance. Like the president of the short-lived republic, which under his leadership had lasted a mere 12 days, many of these notables fled to the mainland. Qiu Fengjia, the vice president stationed at Taizhong, stayed a while longer than Tang and the other evacuees, declaring himself the new president and making noises about continuing to fight to the bitter end on behalf of the republic.[4] But soon Qiu chose safe harbor on the mainland rather than the wrath of the Japanese. Some Taiwanese poets during the Japanese era evolved a favorable mythology concerning Qiu's role in the abortive republic and the resistance effort. But a poet closer to the events of those dismal days penned a more appropriate couplet that circulated among Qiu's followers:

> The Great Minister so recently in power now severs connection to the land.
> In disfavor and without might, the lonely official can return to Heaven.[5]

Bandits wreaked havoc across the island, taking advantage of a period during which the Qing court had pulled its officials from the island and the Japanese had yet to install their administration. As the tide ebbed one day at the port of Lugang, a gentry-merchant named Gu Xianrong facilitated the entrance of the Japanese into this venerable bastion of Taiwanese culture. On

June 7, 1895, the Japanese army took Taibei with no loss of life and, in fact, no bloodshed. It is possible to date the end of the Republic of Taiwan at the time of this event or even earlier, when Tang Jingsong made his escape. But those choosing to identify the Republic of Taiwan with the continuation of the resistance movement have some basis for a claim that the Japanese had not conclusively nixed the idea of independence until mid-October.[6]

Liu Yongfu can be given credit for lending some validity to that view. He proved considerably more dedicated to the resistance than had Tang Jingsong or Qiu Fengjia. In Tainan he set up an administration that issued bank notes and postage stamps and in general showed the aspirations of a central government. His Black Flag forces caused the Japanese to invest considerable military might in the southern regions of Taiwan. Fierce fighting in several places continued throughout the summer and into the early fall before the Japanese were able to tighten the noose. Before he himself was pulled in, though, Liu at last resorted to the familiar route of survival among the leadership that had opposed the Japanese: On October 19, 1895, some 148 days after he and the others had begun their resistance, Liu contravened his previous vow to "live or die with Taiwan." He escaped by ship to Xiamen.[7]

However, the departure of the last of the three main figures of the resistance did not pave the way for a smooth assumption of power by the Japanese. Guerrilla attacks from mountain and other secluded redoubts continued to be a problem for seven years. One major confrontation of June 1896 featured acts of great cruelty on the part of the Japanese, as hundreds were sent to their deaths in what became known as the Yunlin Massacre. A year later Governor-General Nogi Maresuke sought to end the disturbances through a "triple-guard system" that in the end fell far short of quelling the opponents of Japanese rule. During 1898–1903 the Japanese soldiers killed 12,000 Taiwanese resisters who were branded "bandit-rebels" by the colonial regime. This brought the number of Taiwanese deaths in the struggle against the Japanese to about 20,000. By no means did the Japanese themselves escape unscathed; in the effort to pacify the Taiwanese populace, 5,300 Japanese doing the bidding of the colonial government went to their deaths, while another 27,000 were hospitalized. Sporadic shows of resistance would occur throughout the Japanese tenure on Taiwan, but by 1902 the Japanese pacification effort was clearly achieving its aims and the colonial government was on its way to creating very strict mechanisms of control that made coordinated resistance virtually impossible.[8]

Through May 8, 1897, those Taiwanese who chose to do so could leave the island rather than submit to Japanese rule. More than 6,000 people, about 23 percent of Taiwan's population, chose to return to ancestral villages on mainland China rather than live under Japanese authority. Most of the upper gentry chose to leave Taiwan. But 77 percent of the population decided to remain, and among these were lower- and middle-level gentry whom the Japanese would endeavor to co-opt and depend upon heavily in their governance of the island.

Those who remained on the island suffered from an acute identity crisis. Taiwan's history of Han Chinese settlement had never featured any great love between the island's people and the officials of Qing governance. People from village communities had frequently answered the call of local notables who rebelled against Qing rule. The identities of the people of Taiwan lay partly in the ancestral villages of Fujian and Guangdong, but identification with the Qing empire was tenuous. And increasingly, the Han Chinese of Taiwan had become Taiwanese, seeking their fortunes through permanent settlement of the island. Some even intermarried with and carried on mutually beneficial relationships with the aborigines. Others continued to fight the aborigines for territory on which to establish residence and maintain their economically gainful activities. They fought for territory within Taiwan; they defined their existences within the geographical boundaries and in the context of a unique frontier society. Many Taiwanese—gentry, farmers, merchants—felt abandoned by the Qing, which had so swiftly acquiesced to the Japanese demand for Penghu and Taiwan and had evacuated with like speed. With the passing of 5, 10, and then 20 years and more, the people of Taiwan found themselves adjusting their lives to accommodate Japanese rule, even as they expressed an emerging Taiwanese pride in matters of culture, and even as they made eloquent pleas for self-rule within the Japanese empire. For 50 years, the people of Taiwan would be more distant than ever from the great and transforming events taking place on mainland China, instead focusing mainly on the unique restructuring of their own society. And a tough but modern, efficient Japanese colonial regime, not any Chinese government, would have a great deal to say about how Taiwanese society would be restructured and how the Taiwanese people would live their lives during the first half of the twentieth century.[9]

JAPANESE GOVERNMENTAL ADMINISTRATION

Within a year of the Japanese assumption of power on Taiwan, the Diet passed a law that would set the tone for colonial administration of the island. This piece of legislation, rendered as Law 63, gave the governor-general of Taiwan exceptional powers to issue decrees on his own author-ity, as long as they were consistent with general policy guidelines made in Tokyo. The first three governors-general led rather wandering administra-tions, coming and going in rapid succession. A preoccupation with defeat-ing the resistance during those years left the governing authorities little time or energy for creative administrative initiatives. By 1898, though, the resistance had run its main course and the way was clear for a vigorous governor-general to move the colonial administration forward.[10]

Kodama Gentaro, fourth governor-general of Japanese-ruled Taiwan, began a tenure in 1898 that lasted three times as long as the combined reigns of his predecessors. Assisted by an able civil administrator, Goto Shimpei, the new governor-general immediately took actions designed to establish a firm governing apparatus and to maximize the economic gain that the colonial acquisition could bring to the home country. In 1899 the Kodama administration established the Bank of Taiwan. In 1900 weights and measures were standardized. At about the same time, a comprehensive geological survey was conducted to identify Taiwan's chief natural resources. Similarly, investigations were carried out yielding detailed demographic information and identifying precisely the amount of land under cultivation. A concurrent investigation produced the most accurate information to that point in Taiwanese history regarding the level of taxa-tion and the tax-avoidance rate attending cultivated land ownership. The colonial administration secured revenue from the general public through savings accounts conveniently located at post offices. Excise taxes were fixed for a number of items, and the ability of the colonial government to move toward financial independence was further enhanced through monopolies on the sale of opium and the production of and trade in salt, camphor, and tobacco. By 1906, the harbor at Jilong had been vastly improved, establishing a precedent for vigorous efforts to modernize and greatly extend port facilities, roads, and railroad systems. The efforts of the Kodama-Goto administration in the area of health and sanitation greatly reduced the incidence of cholera, smallpox, and bubonic plague. Soon Taibei had a modern public hospital associated with a medical college founded in the capital. Better health, an ever more productive agricultural sector, and increasing social stability contributed to a steady rise in the population of Taiwan. The population of the island stood at 2,650,000 in 1900, at 2,890,485 in 1905, and at 5,962,000 in 1943.[11]

To maintain order and achieve its economic aims, the colonial regime maintained tight control over the island's populace right down to the vil-lage level. The Japanese had long been aware of China's *baojia* system of local security that placed 100 households *(hu)* together in a unit known as a *jia,* and in turn brought 10 *jia* into joint association in a unit called a *bao.* Leaders of each *hu, jia,* and *bao* were carefully identified and a system of mutual responsibility at these levels was put in place. The colonial administration continued to work through the *baojia* system, drawing from its constituent units in establishing local, able-bodied militia *(soteidan* or *zhuangding).* During the years 1898–1909, local notables were carefully identified for leadership of small towns and villages; in the larger towns and cities, ward and section chiefs were installed to administrate government initiatives, to secure community support for the policies of the colonial regime, and to recruit labor for construction projects. To install leaders at these levels of colonial governance, the administration drew heavily from the local gentry and the traditional leaders within the *baojia* system. The colonial regime was highly successful in co-opting local leaders for its own purposes, rewarding them financially, enhancing their prestige with posts bearing both important-sounding titles and real responsibility, and ceremonially awarding their efforts. One of the flashier instances of the latter was Governor-General Nogi's initiative of 1897 through which he bestowed honors on loyal and effective leaders at the local level. He had the leaders brought to the capital at Taibei for an impressive and highly symbolic ceremony during which the colonial regime made its expectations clear and demonstrated its willingness to bestow significant honor on those who rose to its expectations.[12]

For the most part, pacification of the Taiwanese populace had been achieved by 1915, creating a slightly more relaxed atmosphere and leading the governors-general to adopt a more liberal attitude about Taiwanese participation in higher governmental and educational institutions. From about 1915 through the early 1930s, the governors-general were not quite so autocratic as had been the case to date. Two reasons help to explain this fact. First, the governors-general had become more heavily subject to the policies of the central government and the laws passed in the Diet in Tokyo. The passage of a new measure, dubbed Law 3, formalized this policy shift; although it did not overturn Law 63, and the governors-general certainly retained considerable power, the law did have the effect of tying the colonial regime more tightly to the governing institutions of the home country. Second, internal factors contributed to the less-dictatorial style of rule by the governors-general. By the 1920s the colonial regime had been in place on Taiwan for a quarter of a century. The Japanese had gained a greater understanding of the island's people, and the Taiwanese people had adjusted to the requirements and circumstance of colonial rule. The 1920s brought limited self-government through participation of Taiwanese in lower-level government councils. At the island-wide level, there existed a consultative council comprising both Taiwanese and Japanese representatives; the council had little power but did provide some outlet for the expression of Taiwanese opinion. Increasingly, Taiwanese pressure on the colonial regime came not in the form of aggression but in the form of demands for more participation within the colonial context, variously as subjects or citizens within the Japanese empire. Revolutionary-tinged resistance had turned to expressions of desire for greater self-rule within the parameters of Japanese imperial authority. Both the colonial regime and the home government showed some inclination to consider the moderate opinion voiced by leaders of the self-rule movement.[13]

In 1920 came a final reorganization of local government. The establishment of five provinces *(shu)* logically recognized the key regions of cultural and economic coherence on the island; the provincial governments were headquartered in Gaoxiong, Tainan, Taizhong, Taibei, and Jilong. Within each of these provinces were governments for mid-level municipalities *(shi)* and rural counties *(gun)*, as well as those for lower-level townships *(gai)* and villages*(sho)*. Administration for the more sparsely populated and less-developed areas along the east coast and on the Penghu islands accordingly took a different shape. Two subprovinces *(cho)* were established on the east coast, and within these were several branch offices, as well as townships and even smaller administrative sections *(ku)*. On Penghu, the administrative apparatus held a place in the hierarchy just below that of the subprovincial governments and was identified as *hokoto-cho;* within this, too, was a hierarchy of lower-level governments. The reach of the colonial government thus extended way down into the villages and residences of rural Taiwan and brought into the fold of the Japanese administration Taiwanese employees occupying posts at all points along the hierarchy, even taking positions of leadership at the township and village levels. There was a good deal of overlap in the leadership within the *baojia* system and the formal governmental administration. There were strong incentives for locally prominent folk to cooperate with the colonial government, and the gentry in turn were usually able to gain the cooperation of people living within their areas of influence.[14]

By the 1920s, the Taiwanese people could clearly see that although the Japanese were tough and even harsh with those who refused to cooperate with the colonial government, the system that they put in place was rational. Both rewards and consequences flowing from reactions to colonial policy were predictable. There was frank recognition that the colonial regime had brought numerous health, sanitation, and infrastructural improvements to the island.[15] The Taiwanese populace could also see that both the agricultural and industrial sectors of the economy had undergone significant modernization.

ECONOMIC DEVELOPMENT UNDER THE JAPANESE

Surveys taken during the Kodama-Goto administration revealed that Taiwanese soil and mountains contained few gems or minerals that the colonial administration could exploit for economic gain. But the soils of the western coast in particular were rich for agricultural purposes, and the farmers were hardworking and sophisticated in the application of traditional technology. The Japanese administration quickly determined that the chief economic value of the island was in its rice and sugar economy; both of these agricultural commodities would be well received as export items to the home market.[16]

When the Japanese went into the fields to conduct their investigations, the small-rent *(xiaozu)* landlords impressed them with their knowledge of rural conditions and their dominance in local affairs. Deciding that the prevailing two-tiered system had to be simplified for the sake of efficiency, the Japanese administration marked the big-rent *(dazu)* class of landlords for extinction, granting clear title to the *xiaozu* group. The *dazu* group was compensated for its losses: According to an order issued in February 1905, landlords were to receive some combination of seven types of public bonds for forgoing rights to the land. Compensation to landlords owning rice lands varied by region: 5.4 years' worth of rent in the North, 3.8 years' worth of rent in central Taiwan, and about 3 years' worth of rent in the South.[17]

The Japanese administration insisted on formal documentation of landownership on an island frontier where formal documentation on newly opened land and the acquisition of formal titles to the land had not been the regular practice. According to a February 14, 1903, report, 600 land parcels per month were reverting to Japanese ownership. Formerly Taiwaneseowned agricultural land confiscated by the administration was usually sold to Japanese entrepreneurs. By 1939 a Japanese population on Taiwan that represented 5.5 percent of total inhabitants controlled 100,943 *jia,* about 13.3 percent of all cultivated land. In the areas of Gaoxiong (23.4 percent), Taidong (23.9 percent), and Hualian (45.9 percent), the figures were higher still. Sugar was the main interest of Japanese purchasers of land. A report from Hualian in 1926 records that 9,428 *jia*—with 5,000 *jia* of that being cultivated land—was controlled by the Port of Yanshui Sugar Manufacturing Company, Ltd.; the latter figure represented 25 percent of all cultivated land in the Hualian area.[18]

From 1910 to 1914 the colonial administration continued its investigation into the resources of Taiwan with a survey of the forest and wilderness areas, applying the same strict standards of ownership that had been applied in the plains. In the aftermath of the survey the government held 916,775 *jia* of land classified as forest and wilderness; only 56,951 *jia* remained in private Taiwanese hands. At that point, then, the government owned about 94 percent of such lands. The administration opened up 266,399 *jia* of the forest and wilderness land in its possession for sale to private interests and favored Japanese entrepreneurs with extremely low prices. Not surprisingly, Japanese nationals made 85 percent of these land purchases. The administration's land registration and public land sale policies met with violent resistance in some areas, but such resistance was defeated swiftly and surely.[19]

The Japanese colonial government's tax reform policy and land registration efforts greatly increased its tax revenue potential. By 1905, the amount of land subject to taxation was nearly double that in 1897 and total taxes collected had nearly quadrupled. By the time the Kodama-Goto era ended in 1912, the administration had created an efficient government and economic structure for increasing its own revenue and creating an attractive investment climate for Japanese entrepreneurs.[20]

By 1910, having put itself and its nationals in command of the island colony's resources, the Japanese administration began to concentrate its attention on maximizing the value of Taiwan's agricultural wealth. Northern Taiwanese hillsides continued to produce tea leaves; pineapples were grown in a number of areas in the South; and various other crops, poultry, and hogs contributed to Taiwan's agricultural output during the Japanese period. But the colonial administration placed the greatest emphasis by far on those crops that had traditionally been the most important on Taiwan: rice and sugar. Taiwan produced rice on a significantly larger scale than did Korea (also annexed by Japan in 1910); thus, the colonial administration intended to nurture Taiwan's thriving rice economy to supplement Japanese stocks when the demands of a rapidly industrializing, urbanizing economy meant rice shortages at home. Taiwan's proximity to Japan, and Japan's direct control of the island, many of its fields, and almost all of its refining factories, also made the colony an ideal source of sugar for profitable export.[21]

At the heart of Japanese policies to increase rice production in Taiwan were energetic construction of waterworks, the promotion of the *ponlai* rice strain, the founding of an agricultural association with local branches throughout the island, and the founding of a centralized network of stations for conducting research and disseminating results. Rain over much of Taiwan, especially in the South, is concentrated in the summer months. Brief, vicious rains during those months often caused flooding, washed away crops, inundated fields, filled fields with sediment, and buried crops in debris. To minimize damage from floods such as these, which could claim as much as 10 percent of the island's crop, the Japanese energetically set about constructing waterworks in the early twentieth century. Between the years 1907 and 1926 the administration oversaw the construction of 36 dikes or dams covering an area of 39,000 *jia*. The largest water control projects were the Taoyuan and Jianan dams. The Taoyuan dam and reservoir complex, completed in 1928, irrigated an area of 22,000 *jia* in the northern part of the island around Taibei. Completed in 1932, the Jianan dam and reservoir system irrigated 150,000 *jia* of the plain of the same name, located in southwestern Taiwan between Jiayi and Tainan. Throughout Taiwan, irrigated areas and areas protected by dikes and dams in 1932 totaled 527,000 *jia*, a 150 percent increase over 1905. The percentage of all agricultural land benefiting from waterworks rose from 31.1 percent in 1905 to 59.6 percent in 1937, and the amount of wetfield rice land benefiting from systematic irrigation rose from 64 percent to 96.9 percent. This increase in area under systematic irrigation has been credited with generating 60 percent of the increase in rice output from 1922 to 1938.[22]

The widespread use of a new rice strain, *ponlai,* also contributed greatly to rising rice output. In 1922 Taiwanese farmers were producing the traditional *zailai* strain of rice; more than 414,000 hectares were planted in *zailai* that year. But *zailai* rice did not suit the Japanese taste. In the 1920s the Japanese administration sought to create a new variety with potential for export to the home market. The Central Research Institute's agricultural department encouraged local agricultural associations to test the appropriateness of new strains produced by the field laboratories of the institute. By 1926 local observation around the island had yielded a consensus on how to cultivate a new strain that seemed to best fulfill the requirements of high output and export potential. On May 5, 1926, this new variety was named *ponlai* at the Japanese Rice and Grain Conference in Taibei. Only about 400 hectares had been planted in *ponlai* prototypes in 1922, but soon thereafter extension workers accompanied by police provided instruction in planting the new strain. The cultivation area planted in *ponlai* rice rose to 24,000 hectares in 1925; 68,000 hectares in 1926; and 130,000 hectares in 1928, a year in which *ponlai* rice comprised 22.3 percent of all cultivation area given to rice and grain production. By 1944 the cultivation area planted in *ponlai* totaled roughly 400,000 hectares, about 67 percent of the cultivation area planted in rice and other grain.[23]

In addition to the construction of major new waterworks and the successful dissemination of the *ponlai* rice strain, another institutional innovation that greatly aided the Japanese in raising rice production in Taiwan was the agricultural association. The first branch of the colonial regime's Agricultural Association was established in today's Sanxia *zhen* of Taibei *xian* on September 9, 1900. Sanxia had been the site of a rebellion costly in lives and property two months prior to the association's founding; from the beginning, the Japanese conceived the Agricultural Association as a device for local control as well as for disseminating agricultural knowledge. The first branch and a second branch established in April 1901 were disbanded in an administrative restructuring carried out in November of that year. However, the association concept remained a key component of Japanese agricultural policy in Taiwan, and by 1908 Agricultural Association branches were prevalent throughout the island.[24]

During the Japanese period the local branches of the Agricultural Association were under extremely tight control by the central administration in Taibei, which passed directives down through each *zhou* to the smaller administrative units, the *ting* and *zhiting*. All *zhou* offices nominated local landlords and wealthy farmers for Agricultural Association membership, guiding them in establishing local branches and providing them with capital, land, and administrative offices. A close relationship was maintained between the local branches of the Agricultural Association and the *zhou* agricultural experimentation institutes so as to facilitate the dissemination of new crop varieties and agricultural techniques. By 1910 there were on average 7.1 staff members working out of the 87 basic-level *zhiting* branches. These staff members worked through the landlords and wealthy farmers who held exclusive membership in the local branches, and these local notables in turn spread new information, varieties, and techniques to the humbler owner-cultivators and tenant farmers. The Agricultural Association branches were invaluable tools of the colonial administration for solidifying power at the local level and using that power to increase the technical sophistication of agricultural practices throughout the island. Information that came through local agricultural experimentation institutes to the local Agricultural Association branches was coordinated by, and often originated in, the Central Agricultural Research Institute in Taibei. The forerunner of this institute was founded in 1899 and assumed the name given above in 1903. Departments doing research in soil, crop varieties, chemical fertilizers, and livestock disease gave careful attention to the specific agricultural conditions prevailing in Taiwan. The local agricultural experimental institutes passed on the results of this research and also conducted their own research into new crop varieties, fertilizer application, livestock-raising techniques, pest control, and the like. Each branch of the Agricultural Association had an experimental farm for testing the results of the central and local research institutes.[25]

The impressive infrastructure erected by the Japanese for the purpose of increasing rice production in particular and agricultural production in general, together with the hard work of Taiwan's diligent farmers, resulted in the world's first green revolution. Among the improvements that contributed to the revolution were new crop varieties, greater application of chemical fertilizer and more-concentrated applications of farm-produced biological fertilizers, shortened time for nurturing rice seedlings in the seedbed, the dense and strategic planting of trees to serve as windbreaks for cultivated lands, deeper plowing, more-intensive cultivation, and better weeding and pest control techniques. Rice cultivation area on Taiwan more than doubled between 1900 and 1935. Production per *jia* also doubled, so that more than four times as much rice was being produced in 1935 as in 1900.[26]

Much of the rice produced during the Japanese tenure on Taiwan was exported to the Japanese home market. Virtually all rice exported from Taiwan went to Japan. By 1908 exports took 23.3 percent of total rice production, and that percentage rose to 26.5 percent during 1921–25, 34.6 percent during 1926–30, 45.5 percent during 1931–35, and 50.4 percent during 1936–38 before falling back to 40.2 percent during 1939–40. The large amount of rice going for export meant decreased supply in Taiwan and lower consumption of rice for the Taiwanese people. The average annual amount of rice consumed per person during 1936–38 was 23.6 percent less than it had been during 1911–15. Sweet potatoes, considered a much inferior food by the Taiwanese, became a staple for more and more families: The average annual sweet potato consumption per person during the 1936–38 period was 21.1 percent more than it had been during 1921–25. But wartime destruction meant an absolute drop in both rice and sweet potato production and a decline in consumption of such vegetables as carrots, kale, celery, eggplant, and garden peas. Precipitous drops between 1944 and 1945 especially threatened the Taiwanese food supply.

Taiwanese farmers were immensely more productive during the Japanese era than they had been previously, but during the wartime period they ate less of their preferred food, and at times they were hungry.[27]

Whereas meeting the homeland's demand for rice was the colonial administration's major impetus to develop a thriving agricultural economy on Taiwan, there was also substantial profit for Japanese entrepreneurs in developing the sugar economy. In Japan in 1894 the domestic market demand for sugar exceeded supply by a factor of five. In 1900 Japanese entrepreneurs formed the Taiwan Sugar Manufacturing Corporation, Ltd., and established Taiwan's first new-style mechanized sugar-refining factory. The colonial administration encouraged this investment, placing its Taiwan Sugar Affairs Agency in charge of a program to improve sugar cane seeds and to dispense funds heavily subsidizing the sugar industry. It also set stringent requirements for the founding of new sugar-refining factories, specifying the methods to be used in the refining process.[28]

As Japanese entrepreneurs established supremacy in these new-style factories, Taiwanese sugar factories were eclipsed. For the period 1901–02 Taiwanese factories numbered 1,117 and controlled 98 percent of the market. By 1912–13 the number of these factories had declined to 223, with only an 11.8 percent market share. By 1922–23 the number fell to 121, with a mere 1.8 percent market share. By 1927–28 forty-five new-style, Japanese-owned factories controlled 98.2 percent of the market. Figures from the period 1936–37 indicate that 67.7 percent of the market was controlled by four companies: the Taiwan Sugar Company, the Greater Japan Sugar Company, the Meiji Sugar Company, and the Port of Yanshui Sugar Company.[29]

Technological improvements in the production of the raw material that kept these factories in operation were as impressive as they were for rice. The amount of land given to sugarcane cultivation increased from 16,000 jia in 1902 to 150,000 jia in 1918; yields per jia increased 2.3-fold between 1907 and 1937, so that the supply of raw sugarcane to factories rose dramatically. The modern refining processes required by the government raised efficiency in the manufacture of sugar; factory output increased 3.9-fold, faster than the increased production of raw sugarcane per unit of land, between 1907 and 1937. The farmers themselves realized minimal benefit from the increases in raw sugarcane production and refined sugar output. Japanese entrepreneurs established contracts with Taiwanese farmers for the supply of their factories, advancing the farmers loans to cover production costs. After farmers repaid the loans, low prices meant that they had little to show for their efforts, so that the annual cycle of borrowing continued. Entrepreneurs, meanwhile, reaped hefty profits from their mostly export-oriented industry. As with rice, most sugar exports went to the home country.[30]

The growth rates in sugarcane and refined sugar production stimulated the nascent industrialization process during the Japanese tenure on Taiwan. During the 1930s the food industry represented just under 80 percent of all industrial production value, and just over 80 percent of the production value generated by the food industry was claimed by the sugar-refining industry. Most of the remaining production value of the food industry came from pineapple-processing factories. Even nonfood industries were often dependent on or stimulated by the food industries: Factories producing chemicals used sugar by-products; sugar-refining equipment accounted for 64.4 percent of the total value of Taiwan's machine industry; and materials for the canning of pineapples represented 28 percent of the total value of the metal industry. As demand for nonfood industrial products rose during the wartime years of 1937–45, output from textile, machine, metal, and chemical industries rose in production value, but food industries remained dominant right up until the end of the colonial administration in 1945.[31]

The Japanese colonial administration created an infrastructure intended to facilitate growth in these agricultural and industrial economies of Taiwan. Large electricity-generation plants were built. An electrified transportation system was established along the western coast, and a cross-island railroad line and highway were built. Telegraph and telephone networks were constructed. The ports of Gaoxiong and Jilong were modernized. Because most rural communities went without the modern amenities of running water, electricity, telephones, telegraphs, and paved roads, many of these improvements did not touch the lives of the mostly agrarian-based populace very directly. But the infrastructure established by the Japanese did affect strategic areas throughout the island so as to facilitate the movement of goods and messages on an island-wide basis. Likewise, while Japanese established their government offices in Taibei, the traditionally important city of Tainan continued to thrive, and the cities of Gaoxiong, Taizhong, and Jilong underwent considerable growth and development, too. The geographical balance in economic infrastructure and urban growth during the Japanese period would have significant implications for both agricultural and industrial development in the postcolonial era.[32]

Life for farmers during the Japanese period was economically tougher than it had been in previous periods. They received less return on their labors; they ate less well during the wartime years; and, for most, the prospects for advancement of family economic and social status were dimmer. But they lived in healthier, more sanitary conditions, they were better educated, and they had been introduced to significant elements of modernity. The policies and institutions established during the Japanese period would greatly inform economic development in postwar Taiwan.

EDUCATION IN TAIWAN UNDER JAPANESE ADMINISTRATION

Basic literacy came to most of the school-aged populace by the end of the Japanese tenure on Taiwan. School attendance for Taiwanese children rose steadily throughout the Japanese era, from 3.8 percent in 1904 to 13.1 percent in 1917; 25.1 percent in 1920; 41.5 percent in 1935; 57.6 percent in 1940; and 71.3 percent in 1943. Only the sons of landlords and local notables secured spots in middle schools, and even then only about 50 percent of the seats were occupied by Taiwanese; the remainder went to the sons of Japanese residents, who never represented more than 6 percent of the whole population. At the university level, only 20 percent of the students were Taiwanese. For most Taiwanese, male or female, schooling stopped at the end of the third grade, and the minimal literacy in the Japanese language that they had gained would have limited application for those whose lives would unfold mainly in the postcolonial period. Still, Japanese advancement of the ideal of basic universal literacy very well may be credited with increasing Taiwanese receptivity to modern changes in education and other areas of life, as well.[33]

During the early years of Japanese control, the colonial administration put in place a number of common schools *(kogakko)*. These taught the Japanese language to a limited number of Taiwanese children and used it as a medium of instruction. Teachers holding sway in the classroom, and the books that they had the children read, delivered heavy doses of Japanese culture and history to the students and conveyed the essence of the Japanese world view. The schools did offer instruction in the classical Chinese literary language, the language of Confucius and Laozi, which for centuries Chinese and Japanese scholars alike had mastered as an art separate from communication in their particular dialects and spoken vernacular. The schools also placed heavy emphasis on the study of Western subjects: the various modern sciences, history, geography, economics, and literary technique. But throughout the first couple of decades of Japanese rule, most Taiwanese seeking an education attended more traditional Chinese schools *(shobo)* and a significant number of young people were trained in the schools of the Dominicans and the Presbyterians.[34]

A notable shift in the colonial administration's education policy occurred during the reigns of the governors-general Akashi Motojiro (June 1918–October 1919) and Den Kenjiro (October 1919–September 1923). In 1919 came Akashi's imperial rescript on education that, while keeping the segregated system of education intact, indicated a resolve to improve the education of the Taiwanese and especially to offer abundant opportunities for vocational training. Then in 1922 a rescript issued by Den ordered a great expansion of the number of common and primary schools, offering routes to higher education not on the basis of ethnicity but rather of competition in the Japanese language. Of course, not every Taiwanese youngster speaking in Minnan or Hakka or an aboriginal language at home while learning Japanese at school would master Japanese as well as those whose mothers and fathers spoke the language at home. But especially for the children of the local Taiwanese elite, educational opportunities did improve from the 1920s forward. The Japanese encouraged Taiwanese students to pursue studies in education, medicine, engineering, and other vocations and professions that had high practical utility while steering them clear of political controversy. Increasingly greater numbers of Taiwanese students were seen at the middle school level, and from there the more successful and favored ones might move on to studies at the high school level and even gain entrance into the imperial university in Taibei. And a select number of Taiwanese also traveled to, and gained entrance into the universities of, Japan. Local elites from Taiwan first traveled to Japan in 1903, when five hundred of their number attended the Osaka Exhibition. During the years 1903–15 travel to Japan became much in vogue among the Taiwanese elite who had the wherewithal, and the good graces of the colonial masters, to make the trip. The years 1915–22 saw an increasing number of Taiwanese students gaining entrance into the universities of Japan, so that by the latter year 2,400 Taiwanese were undertaking advanced education in the colonial home country. By 1942, this number had increased almost 200 percent: In that year, 7,000 Taiwanese students were matriculating in the institutions of higher education in Japan. And by 1945, as many as 30,000 people of Taiwanese provenance were residing in Japan.[35]

Allowing Taiwanese students to pursue their education in Japan was of course a double-edged sword for colonial policy. On the one hand, such training drew a good many students into the Japanese cultural sphere and strengthened their attachment to and identification with Japan. But Japanese universities of the time were alive with the ideas of the modern world, and in many organizations and at many an informal gathering there arose opportunities to entertain lively discussions on matters pertinent to modernization, imperialism, nationalism, cultural identity, and self-determination. In a phenomenon widely observed in other colonial contexts, a significant number of young Taiwanese studying in Japan began thoughtfully to examine their own identity in the modern world and to evaluate where that identity lay in relation to Japan and to mainland China.[36]

TAIWANESE CULTURE AND THE EMERGENCE OF A TAIWANESE IDENTITY

By the 1920s, a new Taiwanese intelligentsia had already begun to emerge among the island's elite. In March 1920 a group of young intellectuals living and studying in Japan formed the New People's Society *(Shinminaki)* and published a journal known as the *Formosan Youth (Taiwan seinen)*, which was soon renamed *Taiwan People's Journal.* In 1927 its sponsors moved the publication site from Tokyo to Taibei. In 1921 the Taiwanese physician Jiang Weishui formed the Taiwan Cultural Association *(Taiwan bunka kyokai)*, an organization widely credited with launching the Formosan nationalist movement. This organization helped launch a new mode of Taiwanese drama and usher in the New Literature movement, which peaked in 1934. The linguistic medium used by most contributing authors was Japanese, but the writings were rife with the quest for an authentic Taiwanese identity. Closely associated with the literary movement were a growing feminist movement, seeking to overturn the multiple inequities between males and females in the traditional society, and an aggressive agitation for home-rule and the establishment of a Taiwanese parliament. In 1923 came the formation of the League for the Establishment of a Taiwanese Parliament *(Taiwan gikai kisei domeikai)*, which submitted petitions calling for self-rule annually from 1921 through 1934.[37]

Radicals in the Taiwan Cultural Association came to dominate the group by 1927. The leftists generally advocated a Marxist framework for political discussions, and some called for the establishment of a Taiwanese Communist Party. Such radical activist domination led moderates to form a new political organization, the Taiwanese Popular Party *(Taiwan min shuto)*, which advocated not separation from Japan or condemnation of the colonial regime as a variant of world imperialism and capitalist exploitation, but rather universal suffrage and self-government within the empire. Dissatisfaction with the Japanese response, though, moved the majority membership of the Taiwanese Popular Party toward more radical ideas and into more radical modes of expression. Meanwhile, the stalwart conservatives of the Taiwanese Popular Party formed the Taiwanese Federation for Local Autonomy *(Taiwan chihojichi renmei)*. But municipal elections in 1935 proved disappointing to those seeking to advance the candidacies of people willing to act with some independence in pushing for self-rule within the colonial regime. In 1934 the Japanese administration had shut down all organizations of a leftward bent; in the face of the electoral disappointments of 1935, and understanding the shift of the political wind, even the moderate Federation for Local Autonomy disbanded in August 1937.[38]

The war years were on. Life on the island was about to become tougher in many ways. Yet, during the years of the Taiwanese self-rule movement and the development of a radical political fringe, practitioners of the literary arts had made their own highly significant contributions to the discussion of Taiwanese identity. First came a movement that paralleled the modernist push on mainland China to use the modern vernacular and Western literary forms to express ideas regarding a venerable old civilization facing the pressures of life in the twentieth century. Thus, the initial agenda of the Taiwanese Cultural Association had both cultural and political components. On the one hand, there was a push to bring Taiwan into the modern world of vernacular usage and literary expression, just as Hu Shi, Lu Xun, Guo Moro, Lao She, Bing Xin, and many others were so advocating on the mainland. But there was also a push to focus on problems unique to Taiwan and to examine what the circumstances of history, including those of colonial life, had wrought for the Taiwanese people. Authors such as Lai Ho (1894–1943), Chen Xugu (1896–1965), and Cai Qiutong (b. 1900) were pioneers in this cultural quest and the use of Western literary forms. Many of these writers had been educated in traditional Chinese schools and remained more comfortable with the Chinese language. They tended to produce their literary works in Chinese while offering ideas that condemned the old society and advanced the case for modernity in highly favorable terms.[39]

In 1920 Taiwanese expatriates in Tokyo launched the Taiwanese New Culture Movement *(Taiwan xin wenhua yundong)* through the founding of the New People Association *(Xinmin hui)*. Another organization closely associated with the movement was the Taiwanese Youth Organization *(Taiwan qingnian hui)*. The literary energy of such groups soon produced the journal, *New Youth (Taiwan qingnian)*. Evidencing many affinities with the New Culture Movement on the mainland, the version on Taiwan demonstrated antifeudal, anti-Confucian attitudes; a propensity to accept the tenets of social Darwinism; and a yearning for national emancipation frequently coming through the ideological filter of socialism or communism. The intellectuals dominant at this early stage of the Taiwanese New Literature and New Culture movements felt the pressure exerted by Social Darwinist ideas, and under the immediacy of the struggle of nations for dominance sought to move Taiwan forward toward sociocultural modernization, assuming that Western forms generally meant more-enlightened outlooks. There was also a manifestly anti-imperialist attitude, expressed in terms calling for national salvation or the end of colonialism. In 1924 the poet Zhang Wojun launched an attack on traditional poets, provoking an energetic debate that came to be known as the New vs. Old Literary Debate *(xinjiu wenxue lunzhan)* that raged between 1924 and 1926. Although the debate was not entirely settled, the New Literature was legitimized as a powerful social institution.[40]

Zhang Wojun had been a student at Peking Normal University, where he and others came under the influence of Hu Shi, Chen Duxiu, Lu Xun, Guo Moro, Bing Xin, Wang Luyen, and Ling Shuhua. But on Taiwan, dependency on the ideas of mainland writers soon ran its course and discussion came to focus on other momentous issues aired in the Nativist Literary Debate *(xiangtu wenxue lunzhan)* that raged during 1931–32.

Huang Shihui was a dominant figure in this debate. He advocated a proletarian literature focused on the problems of the working class and called for a literature set in Taiwan, dealing with issues of direct relevance to the island's people, written with a Taiwanese consciousness, and rendered in the Minnan vernacular. The challenge presented by the latter notion dominated another phase in the early stages of the New Literature Movement. This issue was hot in the year 1932, calling forth the Taiwanese Language Debate *(Taiwan hua wen lunzhan)*. In this phase of the ongoing debates, Yang Shouyou (1905–59) was a chief force, penning numerous articles for the *Taiwanese People's Newspaper (Taiwan minbao)*. Some writers such as Yang and his influential contemporary Lai Ho attempted to use their native Minnan dialect, historically only a spoken language, as a tool of literary expression. Lai's short story, "A Comrade's Letter of Criticism" *(Yige tongzhih bixin)*, represented one such effort but also proved so exhausting that Lai subsequently made few similar attempts. Under strictures imposed by the Japanese, the language of the colonials was soon mandated as the exclusive language of literary production. But whatever the success in adapting Minnan for literary usage, the very attempt said a great deal about an emerging Taiwanese consciousness and confirmed the journey of Taiwanese New Literature down a path quite divergent from that trodden by mainland writers.[41]

The first generation of writers to publish their work in the journals of the Taiwanese New Literature were well versed in classical Chinese and competent in writing traditional Chinese poetry. They played a historical role as new intellectuals intent on breaking with the past and casting their social visions toward the future. They viewed society in intensely moral terms, used an omniscient narrative style, and gave their works episodic plot structures; these were carryovers from the Chinese vernacular tradition put to work in the modern short story, novel, and free verse. There was an artificial quality about much of what came from this generation. Then a second generation of writers increasingly made their voices heard. These included Yang Kui (b. 1906), Chen Huochuan (b. 1908), Wen Nao (b. 1908), Zhang Wenhuan (b. 1909), Long Yingzong (b. 1911), Lu Horo (b. 1914), and Wang Changxiong (b. 1916). Beginning around 1933 these and other Taiwanese writers tended to favor Japanese as their medium of expression, and from about mid-1936 almost no Chinese was used by Taiwanese writers publishing in the literary journals of the time. These writers were raised in a more modern society than the older generation had known, and most had studied in Japan. They entered university classes, frequented salons, and entered contests. Winning the latter could launch or greatly boost careers, as witnessed in the careers of mid-1930s winners Yang Kui, Lu Horo, and Long Yingzong. Such writers had a much firmer grasp of Western artistic concepts than did the older writers, rendering their works in that mode ironically through the medium of the Japanese language. A diversity of social visions could be seen in the writers of these works. Yang Kui held to a more orthodox leftism, wheras Zhang Wenhuan exuded a humanistic liberalism. Lu Horo wrote in a naturalistic style that tended to focus on typical characters drawn especially from the Taiwanese gentry. Stories by Yang and Lu revealed a fervent anti-imperialism; rendered in the Japanese language, the stories could be taken as metaphors for the ambivalent Taiwanese cultural position. Taiwanese culture was not Chinese mainland culture and had arguably become much more than a mere Chinese variant. It reflected a Japanese influence with which it had been forced to come to terms. Although critical of the Japanese as imperialists, the writers of the Taiwanese New Literature used the Japanese language and embraced Western forms that had traversed a literary and cultural pipeline through Japan. Already posing challenges to the definition of Taiwanese society and culture, the Japanese presence and the long severance from the major events taking place on the mainland became ever more acute under the conditions of wartime Taiwan.[42]

THE FINAL YEARS OF JAPANESE RULE

With the emphasis on the southward advance *(nanshin)* into the Pacific and Southeast Asia after 1937, the Japanese increasingly used Taiwan as a staging area for forays into places targeted for conquest. From Taiwan, the Japanese launched successful conquests of Canton (late 1938) and Hainan (February 1939). The Taiwan strait passed to exclusive Japanese control during 1940, and in the latter part of that year Governor-General Hasegawa Kiyoshi became the point man in the ambition to establish a Greater East Asia Co-Prosperity Sphere *(Dai Toa Kyoeiken)*. After the December 7, 1941, attack on Pearl Harbor came intensive preparations for the decisive conflict looming in the Pacific, during which Taiwan served as the key staging area for a successful attack on Luzon (concluded in May 1942) and then for the successful move into Burma and on to the border with India. But the tide began to turn in the Asian-Pacific theater during 1943–44, and by the end of 1944 Taiwan's people had to forbear U.S. forces' aerial attacks aimed at key industrial, port, and military installations.[43]

Creation of major industrial installations on Taiwan originated in the decisions made in a major conference of 1935, held in Taibei. At this gathering Taiwan was designated as the location for plants that would process bauxite, iron ore, crude oil, and rubber from Malaya and the islands of the Indonesian archipelago. A decision was made to improve a number of harbors to serve as additional seaports and to build more electricity-generating facilities. In 1938 an Industrial Commission met in Taibei, laying plans for greater electrification of the towns and cities of the island, for more elaborate transportation networks, for the upgrading of mining operations, and for major improvements in prime industries. The plans laid by the commission did indeed bring massive new hydroelectric installations, new harbors, and impressive new industrial complexes such as the Japanese Aluminum Company plants at Hualian and Gaoxiong.[44]

From 1895 through the 1920s, Taiwan had served as an agricultural appendage of the home country, exploited for the vast amounts of sugar and rice turned out by the Taiwanese farmer vanguards of the green revolution. By the mid-1920s food processing and other light industry had come to occupy important roles in the colonial economy. Taiwanese people with capital and entrepreneurship operated many of the food-processing, handicraft, and other local industries. Then after the eventful year of 1937 came the advent of heavy industry on Taiwan, financed by Japanese investment. To meet the needs of an expanding wartime economy, the colonial regime established new banking and credit institutions. Newly established industrial and financial concerns eventually attracted major involvement from the huge Japanese conglomerates *(zaibatsu)*. By 1935 Taiwan's 7,000 factories employed 68,000 factory workers; and by mid-1943 there were 147,000 skilled factory workers, another 67,000 employees in other nonagricultural operations, and over 200,000 Taiwanese people employed in construction or serving in the military. Urban centers grew rapidly, and elementary and vocational schools sprouted up in many new locations. An effort was made to secure the loyalty of the Taiwanese populace by giving them a vision of honor and prestige within Greater Japan.[45]

Accordingly, the Patriotic Youth Corps *(Hokoku sentai)* was founded in April 1940, followed by the creation of the Imperial Subjects Public Service Association *(Komin hokokai)* a year later. These organizations came into being to guide the imperialization *(kominka)* movement that penetrated all geographical areas and was aggressively promoted in all schools, factories, occupations, and societies. In June 1945 a volunteer corps *(giyu-tai)* was formed under the stress of fading Japanese hopes in the Asia-Pacific War. Throughout the early 1940s, an intensified *kominka* program filled schools and newspapers with propaganda urging people to cast their futures and fortunes with the Japanese empire. A good many Taiwanese answered the call to military service in the Japanese army and navy. By 1945, Taiwan had supplied Japan with 80,433 servicemen and another 126,750 civil employees. Military service was listed in propaganda sheets as the first of "three great obligations"; payment of taxes and diligence in acquiring an education rounded out the list. To facilitate the acquisition of education, the government undertook significant expansion of educational facilities from 1937 to 1945. From 1943 attendance in schools from primary on up was compulsory, and by 1944 three out of four children were enrolled in primary schools. In an atmosphere of fervent wartime nationalism, the government fastidiously implemented an increasingly Japanized curriculum in all schools. Similarly, the colonial regime promoted Shintoism ever more vigorously during the last years of its rule; some local temples were demolished, but more typically an effort was made to locate Taiwanese deities within the Shinto system, thus extending the *kominka* policy to the very gods of the Taiwanese.[46]

Some Taiwanese intellectuals wrote for the war effort. Only one Chinese-language magazine, *Wind and Moon (Feng yue bao)*, lasted as late as 1937. The writers of the Taiwanese nativist movement were kept under tight rein, while authors such as Zhou Jinbo (b. 1920) and Chen Huochuan (b. 1908) cranked out short stories (e.g., Zhou's "The Volunteer Soldier" *[Zhiyuan bing]* and Chen's "The Way" *[Dao]*) serving the propaganda aims of the colonial administration. Many unabashed propagandistic poems and plays flowed from the pens of Taiwanese writers. But members of the Taiwanese New Literature Movement persevered as long as they could. Prior to its forced merger with *Literary Taiwan* in 1941, the journal *Taiwanese Literature* published the most important works of the second-generation Taiwan nativist writers. These included "Capon" *(Yenji)* and "Night Monkeys" *(Yeyuan)* by Zhang Wenhuan; "Wealth, Offspring, and Longevity" *(Caizishou)*, "Peace for the Entire Family" *(Hojia pingan)*, and "Guava" *(Shiliu)* by Lu Horo; "A Village without Doctors" *(Wu yi cun)* by Yang Kui; and "Rapid Torrents" *(Benliu)* by Wang Changxiong. The authors of these works mounted vigorous responses to the colonial bias of *Literary Taiwan* and employed realistic description rather than the romantic language of the journal patronized by the regime. The leftward-leaning stories that appeared in *Taiwanese Literature* focused on local customs, rural life, and folk traditions and so registered resentment against the Japanese imperialists.[47]

People on the beautiful island and the unique historical entity of Taiwan gave evidence of deep division, both among themselves and within individual souls, as the colonial era came to an end. Some people saw Taiwan cloaked in its potential for independence, within the Japanese imperialist realm or otherwise. Some people had come to identify closely with the colonial regime and reaped material rewards and places of honor under Japanese governance. Some people, weary from war and economically depressed, wanted change in whatever form it took. Although ambivalent once they learned of the prospect of governance by another Chinese regime from the mainland, not many Taiwanese knew much about the Guomindang party that came to rule the island at war's end, nor found much to admire during the first five years of its rule.

NOTES

1. Zhou Mingfeng, *Taiwan jian shi* [A concise history of Taiwan] (Taibei: Qian Wei Press, 1994), p. 62; Qi Jialin, *Taiwan shi* [The history of Taiwan], vol. 2 (Taibei: Zili Evening News, 1992), pp. 146–47.

2. Zhou Mingfeng, pp. 62–63; Qi Jialin, pp. 146–47; Huang Dashou, *Taiwan shi gang* [An outline history of Taiwan] (Taibei: Sanmin Book Company, 1982), pp. 206–9.

3. Zhou Mingfeng, pp. 65–66; Qi Jialin, pp. 148–49; Huang Dashou, p. 211.

4. Zhou Mingfeng, pp. 66–67; Huang Dashou, p. 215.

5. Zhou Mingfeng, p. 67.

6. Ibid.; Qi Jialin, pp. 148–49.

7. Zhou Mingfeng, p. 67; Qi Jialin, p. 153; Huang Dashou, pp. 218–25.

8. Zhou Mingfeng, p. 76; Qi Jialin, pp. 154–62; Huang Dashou, pp. 225–29.

9. Zhou Mingfeng, pp. 165–200, provides an appendix with numerous literary documents that express a uniquely Taiwanese dedication to the home island, revealing the emergence of a Taiwanese identity in the course of the nineteenth and twentieth centuries.

10. Zhou Mingfeng, p. 78; Huang Dashou, pp. 232–33 and 296–304.

11. Harry Lamley, "Taiwan under Japanese Rule, 1895–1945: The Vicissitudes of Colonialism," in Murray Rubinstein, ed., *Taiwan: A New History* (Armonk, NY: M. E. Sharpe, 1999), p. 210; Zhou Mingfeng, pp. 79–81.

12. Harry Lamley, p. 225.

13. Ibid., p. 222.

14. Ibid., p. 225.

15. In Tainan County (Guantian District, Shezi Village, Liushuang Hamlet), my own field experiences of talking to people of various ages revealed interesting generational differences as to views of the Japanese. The eldest generation of people who were in their seventies and above around 1990 tended to remember the Japanese more favorably for the improvements they made on Taiwan in the areas of health, sanitation, and public cleanliness.

16. Qi Jialin, pp. 181–82 and 185–87; Huang Dashou, pp. 231–42; and Wu Congxian, *Zhongguo nongye fazhan* [Chinese agricultural development] (Taibei: Central Research Documents Agency, 1984), pp. 507–12.

17. Qi Jialin, p. 185; Wu Congxian, pp. 507–12.

18. Qi Jialin, pp. 185–87.

19. Ibid., pp. 187–90; Huang Dashou, pp. 237–47.

20. Qi Jialin, p. 184.

21. Qi Jialin, pp. 191–204 and 206–11; Huang Dashou, pp. 243–44; Lin Zhongxiong, *Taiwan jingji fazhan sishi nian* [Forty years in the economic development of Taiwan] (Taibei: Zili Evening News, 1987), p. 27.

22. Qi Jialin, pp. 191–93; Huang Dashou, pp. 239–40; Lee Teng-hui, *Taiwan nongye fazhan jingji fenxi* [Economic analysis of the agricultural development of Taiwan] (Taibei: Lianjing Publications, 1980), pp. 200–2; Lin Zhongxiong, p. 22.

23. Qi Jialin, pp. 193–95; Huang Dashou, pp. 243–44.

24. Qi Jialin, pp. 195–97; Huang Junjie, *Taiwan nongye di huanghun* [The twilight of Taiwanese agriculture] (Taibei: Zili Evening News, 1988), p. 202; Wu Congxian, pp. 415–17.

25. Qi Jialin, pp. 196–98; Wu Congxian, p. 402 and pp. 415–17.

26. Qi Jialin, p. 200.

27. Ibid., pp. 202–3.

28. Ibid., pp. 207–8.

29. Ibid., pp. 207–8.

30. Qi Jialin, p. 209; Lin Zhongxiong, p. 27.

31. Qi Jialin, pp. 212, 215, and 216–22; Lin Zhongxiong, p. 29.

32. Qi Jialin, p. 213; Huang Dashou, pp. 236–47; and Lin Zhongxiong, p. 27.

33. Qi Jialin, pp. 227–31. Huang Dashou, pp. 251–288, details the system of education under the Japanese colonial administration. A third-grade education was typical of people in the village of Shezi (Tainan County), where I did research in 1988–90.

34. Lamley, pp. 210–11.

35. Ibid., pp. 230–31.

36. Huang Dashou, pp. 286–96.

37. Lamley, p. 223; Zhou Mingfeng, pp. 86–87; Huang Dashou, pp. 304–12.

38. Lamley, p. 234; Zhou Mingfeng, p. 87.

39. Sung-sheng Yvonne Chang, "Taiwanese New Literature and the Colonial Context: A Historical Survey," in Murray Rubenstein, ed., *Taiwan: A New History* (Armonk, N.Y.: M.E. Sharpe, 1999), pp. 261–74.

40. Ibid., pp. 265–66.

41. Ibid., pp. 266–68. Huang Dashou, pp. 312–19, offers a detailed summary of the Taiwanese New Culture Movement.

42. Chang, pp. 261–74.

43. Lamley, p. 235.

44. Ibid., pp. 236–38.

45. Ibid., pp. 238–42.

46. Ibid., p. 241.

47. Chang, pp. 272-73.

Chapter 6

GUOMINDANG RULE, 1945–2000

Five months after the November 1943 Cairo conference, at which the Allies agreed that Taiwan would come under Guomindang control upon Japan's surrender in the Asia-Pacific War, the Guomindang government in Chongqing (Chungking) established the Taiwan Investigation Committee. The Guomindang government, representing the Republic of China, had been founded and centered in Nanjing in 1912 when the Qing dynasty fell but was forced to move to Chongqing in 1938 under pressure of Japanese victories along the eastern coast of China. Former Fujian governor Chen Yi was chosen to head the Taiwan Investigation Committee, and under Chen's authority one thousand "half-mountain" Taiwanese helped him prepare to exercise governmental authority on the island of their birth. The half-mountain appellation was applied to those native Taiwanese who allied themselves with the Guomindang and gave their efforts to the struggle against the Japanese on the mainland. The Japanese emperor called a halt to his nation's war effort on August 15, 1945, and on September 2, 1945, he signed the official documents of surrender. Through September and October, Guomindang government officials and military personnel arrived on Taiwan to establish mainland Chinese governing authority for the first time since the Qing dynasty relinquished control of the island in 1895.[1]

Most Taiwanese people had supported the Japanese war effort. More than 200,000 Taiwanese had served in the Imperial Navy or the Imperial Army, and some 30,000 Taiwanese had died in that effort. Many of the island's people had embraced the Japanese vision of a united Greater East Asia and looked forward to rising citizenship status within the empire. Such people experienced political disorientation at the turn of events that brought the Asia-Pacific War to a close; some moved to Japan while others scrambled to reorient their loyalties in deference to the reality of Guomindang authority. Many a collaborator suddenly turned enthusiastic Chinese patriot. Some laid low. But there were also those of Han Chinese ethnicity on Taiwan who had yearned for the exit of the Japanese and the institution of a government headed by people closer to their provenance. Overall the Taiwanese masses, war-weary, eager for the normality of peacetime, and hoping for better economic conditions, generally accepted the change in administration and prepared to greet their fellow Han Chinese. Most members of the Taiwanese elite, so recently cooperative with the colonial administration, offered their assistance to smooth the transition. Great disturbance of the social order was contrary to their class interests.[2]

Chen Yi became chief administrator *(xingzheng zhangguan)* of the Taiwan Provincial Executive Office; he also held the title of Taiwan garrison commander, with broad powers and responsibility for civil administration, military oversight, judicial proceedings, and regulatory agencies. There was much to be done. A sizable portion of the carefully built infrastructure established by the Japanese had been laid to waste by American bombs. Inflation raged, the agricultural economy was depressed, non-farm jobs were scarce, and consumer goods were in short supply. Malaria, leprosy, and bubonic plague brought misery to many people across the island. Unfortunately, Chen and his cronies engaged in personal aggrandizement and corruption rather than tackling the considerable problems vexing the people who looked to them for leadership. Back in Chongqing, Chen had already determined that he would favor state control of enterprises over private investment. Accordingly, the state took control of major industrial enterprises, granted monopolies to favored officials, confiscated formerly Japanese private as well as government property, and created trade bureaus to manage mainland and international trade.[3]

As it became clear that the Chen Yi administration had neither the will nor the program to address the serious problems faced by Taiwanese society, hope faded and a deep anger at the new administration set in. Within just a few weeks, the most generally held view was that Guomindang rule brought all of the harshness of Japanese administration without any of its efficiency, predictability, and order. This made the imposition of a new language and prescribed literature in the areas of education and culture all the harder to bear. In the interests of cultural reconstruction, the Taiwan Office of Translation and Compilation promoted mainland Chinese literature and established Mandarin as the official language of the island. Young people, at school and in such organizations as the Three Principles of the People Youth Corps, received heavy doses of Guomindang ideology. But the ideal of nationalism was problematic given the strained identity of a recently colonized people, and the Guomindang showed no interest whatsoever in democracy and the people's livelihood. A tough joke, the effect of which was achieved through the wordplay in homophones typical of the Chinese language, circulated that *san min zhuyi,* the supposed "Three Principles of the People," were really *canmin zhuyi,* "cruel personism." In allegorical expression, people said that the vicious dogs (Japanese) might have been chased away, but slovenly pigs (Guomindang officials) had replaced them.[4]

The Guomindang did establish institutions that gave some scope for Taiwanese opinion. Elections were held in 1946 for village and town councils, county and city councils, and a Provincial Consultative Assembly. But virtually all important posts in the Chen Yi administration went to mainlanders. Even at the county level only 3 of 23 *xian* magistrates were Taiwanese. Members of the Taiwanese elite, who had made a genuine effort to offer their expertise to the incoming administration, were most frequently shunted aside as the influx of officials from the mainland increased each year prior to the Guomindang loss of the mainland to the communists in 1949. In all, 28,000 officials arrived on Taiwan, displacing many of those Taiwanese whose professional lives had been spent in government service. The Guomindang, though, was contemptuous of that service in the colonial administration of the hated Japanese, disparaged the experience acquired during the days of colonial control, and spoke and wrote often about the Japanization *(ribenhua)* and "slavization" *(nuhua)* that plagued Taiwanese who aspired to take their places in the new Chinese administration. As it became clear that the councils and assemblies formed with the elections of 1946 were at best consultative organizations that held no true decision-making power, articulate members of the Taiwanese began to protest their greatly circumscribed role. As the corruption and ineptitude of the Guomindang administration became apparent, these protests increasingly became a demand for self-government for the Taiwanese people on the unique political entity that was their island.[5]

Included among the protesters were half-mountain Taiwanese who might have been expected to be the firmest supporters of the new administration. In response to the contemptuous characterizations of the Guomindang, well-educated and deeply experienced half-mountain Taiwanese such as Li Wanzhu and Song Feiru took issue with the term *slave* to describe the Taiwanese experience under the Japanese. The half-mountain Taiwanese were quick to emphasize the resistance that accompanied the Japanese arrival on the island, the uprisings that continued even after 1902, the assertions of Taiwanese aspirations for self-government, and the literary quest for a Taiwanese identity. A number of these leaders came to suggest that the Guomindang was worse than the Japanese colonial government, which for all of its harshness at least could be depended upon to mete out stiff penalties for definite offenses and in many other ways provide for an orderly, healthy, clean, modernizing society. The Guomindang seemed starkly backward by comparison. Its representatives seemed less interested in the dispensation of good government than they did in satisfying their "five cravings": plenty of gold, luxurious automobiles, government rank, fine homes, and beautiful women. Wang Tiandeng urged that the Guomindang might as well forget the exalted notions expressed in the Three Principles of the People. "Just give us a little law," he said. Zheng Fengyuan availed himself of the wordplay that flows from the tonality and homonym-laden Chinese dialects: In return for their willingness to *jieshou* ("receive") the Guomindang as well-intentioned fellow Chinese, the Taiwanese had become subject to *jieshou* ("plunder") by their new overlords.[6]

Other thoughtful Taiwanese joined in the criticism of the new administration. The attacks came in articles written for the official newspapers and in speeches made in the consultative assemblies. Though the latter lacked true power, they did provide scope for the expression of Taiwanese opinion. Xie Nanguang asserted that Taiwan, so much more developed than the Chinese mainland, was ready to serve as a model province leading the way toward the realization of Sun Yat-sen's Three Principles of the People. Qiu Niantai cited the Taiwanese resistance movement that greeted the colonial masters after the Qing rulers gave away the island to the Japanese; the latter, he said, had at least substantially modernized this key territory of their empire, bringing a level of material progress to the island's people that few on the mainland could even imagine. Leaders such as Li Chunqing, Lin Xiantang, and Guo Guoji lent their pens and voices to the call for self-government. Some even used language that suggested that the best future for Taiwan lay in its recognition as an independent nation. As the inept Guomindang administration declined in favor among the Taiwanese people, articulate Taiwanese voices referenced the economic development and self-rule movement of the Japanese era to assert the need and the right for a high degree of self-government in the postwar world.[7]

Then came the dawning of February 28, 1947, a portentous day in Taiwanese history. The turmoil of a day destined to lodge forever in the consciousness of the Taiwanese people had its origin in an event of the previous evening, when a middle-aged woman selling black market cigarettes was arrested and roughly handled by Guomindang police outside the railroad station in Taibei. Many Taiwanese, elite and non-elite alike, already harbored great ill will against the Guomindang government. More important to most Taiwanese than the goal of self-government espoused by the elite was the simple hope of survival because the Guomindang had by the winter of 1947, lost control of the economy. Rice prices rose so precipitously that on February 14 the rice market had closed indefinitely. Hoarding and black markets had become a way of life. Thugs identified with the Guomindang government stole from the people with abandon. They meted out the most brutal punishment when their actions were met with protest, and there was no recourse in courts of law. Not even the years of wartime dislocation under the Japanese had given evidence of the degree of uncertainty, unpredictability, and economic devastation that now plagued Taiwanese society. A crowd that had gathered on that fateful February 27 felt the impact of this situation deeply, and many could suppress their rage no more. They taunted the Guomindang police, called them names, and threw rocks and whatever else was handy. The police shot into the crowd, killing several and wounding others. Soon Taibei was rife with street demonstrations, and talk in many quarters bespoke large-scale protest and even civil war.[8]

The Taibei City Council convened an urgent meeting. Its members demanded that the offending police in the railroad station incident be jailed immediately and that appropriate punishment be meted out. In communication with the council, Chen Yi seemed contrite and open to taking whatever action was necessary to calm the city. Angry crowds had stormed the main police station and taken over a number of government offices in Taibei. A February 28th Incident Settlement Committee issued a forceful demand for self-government. On March 6 the committee issued a document featuring 32 demands that, if met, would transform the governing authority of Taiwan, bringing a degree of self-government that would make the island polity essentially independent of mainland and Guomindang control. Chen Yi, already backing away from his earlier conciliatory stance, was furious. Some among the half-mountain leadership tried to mediate, and moderates among the self-government advocates sought to scale down the rhetoric and even the substance of the demands. But radicals saw in the unfolding events an opportunity for thoroughgoing change that they wanted to press to full advantage.[9]

Nor was the spirit of rebellion limited to the capital city. Networks of intellectuals and leaders throughout the island brought demonstrations in towns and cities across Taiwan. Now was the time, they thought, to assert the rights and the dignity of the Taiwanese people, to seize the moment to define for the first time in the island's history of Han Chinese inhabitation what it meant to be Taiwanese and what characteristics described the island polity of Taiwan. Tracts were written. Speeches were given. Meetings were held. Government offices were seized, and hope ran high. Then, on March 8, 1947, Guomindang troop reinforcements landed on the island.[10]

They exhibited an efficiency and sense of purpose that the governmental administration itself had not heretofore shown. Chen Yi declared martial law and unleashed an orgy of indiscriminate shooting. On March 13 the authorities inaugurated a movement to exterminate traitors by clearing villages *(qing xiang)* of those suspected not only of having caused trouble but also those merely thought capable of stirring up opposition to Guomindang rule. Collectively the show of real opposition to the Guomindang government and the harsh government response to it became terminologically linked as the February 28th Incident *(er er ba shijian)*. Estimates of the exterminated go as high as 100,000. A commonly held view among the Taiwanese is that about 20,000 went to their deaths, but some cautious scholars say that the figure may have been 10,000 killed and another 30,000 wounded. What is certain is that a brutal and corrupt regime—the island representative of the bungling party on the mainland that was in the midst of badly losing a war it should have won—sent thousands and perhaps tens of thousands of rebels and innocent Taiwanese people to premature reunions with their ancestors.[11]

In a fashion all too similar to the ruthless suppression of popular expression by the governments of modern mainland China, the Guomindang government squeezed the life out of the opposition and then told the big lie. The causes of the February 28th Incident, the new imperialists claimed, were a misunderstanding of the Motherland and the poisonous Japanese legacy. Criminals, youth with Japanese training, Japanese still found here and there around Taiwan, communists, and the "evil politicians" of the Taiwanese elite were to blame. Few were left to take issue in a frank and open manner; the bravest, best, brightest, and most dedicated among those in a position to exercise leadership in behalf of the Taiwanese people had been exterminated or placed under arrest. Farmers and other working people kept their feelings to themselves for fear of reprisal. None would forget, but it would take some time before the memories resurfaced in the marketplace of ideas and free expression. For the next several decades the Guomindang regime would be surprisingly successful in establishing a lively marketplace of the more conventional kind, riveting the attention of a politically suppressed people on goals that they could realistically achieve in the service of the family, the ancestors, and the generations to come. Political participation was dangerous, they had learned. Economic prosperity would be a more realizable aim.[12]

In the aftermath of the February 28th Incident and the latter years of the 1940s, the Guomindang first acted to secure control and reestablish social order. On April 22, 1947, the Guomindang official Wei Daoming replaced Chen Yi, who was recalled to a post in Zhejiang province. Wei made some conciliatory gestures. He lifted martial law, concluded the *qing xiang* campaign of ferreting out opposition, removed communications controls, and attempted a currency reform to curb inflation. He created a Provincial Committee that included 7 Taiwanese among its 15 members. A newly established Taiwanese Provincial Health Department helped to bring plague and cholera under control by 1949. Wei's government demonstrated greater tolerance on the issue of speaking Japanese. The new chief administrator announced that he wanted to move Taiwanese society "from stability to prosperity."[13]

Wei's demeanor, personal style, and smattering of concrete policies helped to relax somewhat the still very tense atmosphere that hung over the island. But there was no longer any doubt that the self-government notion and the expression of any sort of dissent were dead. Wei's government promulgated the "Temporary Provisions Effective during the Period of Mobilization for Suppression of the Communist Rebellion," under which migration and even travel were restricted. An island-wide campaign to register households on government records was carried out in the course of 1947–49 and identification cards were distributed. To prevent public recognition or demonstrations at the anniversary of a painfully remembered event, a new round of arrests took place in February 1948. An editorial in a government paper (no others were allowed) explained the difference between *opposing* and *commenting on* the government. The former involved questioning the legitimacy of the Guomindang regime and implied systemic change; this was considered traitorous. The latter offered a view or views concerning particular problems or the integrity of individual public officials; this was permissible when the goal was clearly to make the system function more efficiently and honestly. This was of course consistent with a view that Chinese communist leader Mao Zedong was to espouse regarding contradictions among the people. As a Leninist party, the Guomindang had origins similar to those of its communist competitor. For at least two decades, even the bravest critics on Taiwan (much like critics living under the Chinese Communist Party on the mainland) would couch their criticisms in terms that arguably fell within the boundaries established by the government.[14]

Any remnant of hope for self-government faded from the realm of possibility when a crony of Chiang Kai-shek, Chen Cheng, replaced Wei Daoming as chief administrator of the Guomindang regime on Taiwan. Under Chen's administration, the Taiwan Provincial Local Self-Government Association became an increasingly mainlander-dominated agency that in fact sought to suppress genuine self-government. Taiwanese representatives such as Huang Chaoqin, the half-mountain chair of the Provincial Consultative Assembly, were forced to focus more and more on the distribution of rewards within the system. A few critics with unusual bases of popular support, such as Li Wanzhu (vice chair of the Provincial Consultative Assembly) and Guo Guoji (Provincial Consultative Assembly representative from Gaoxiong), might test the patience of the government more than others, but even they stayed just within bounds. Liao Wenyi (Thomas Liao), an advocate for Taiwanese independence, and Lin Xiantang, a former supporter of mainland Chinese governance, elected to emigrate to Japan. They could see no future for themselves under a regime that launched a virulent campaign of "White Terror" in 1949 that effected an even more thorough silencing of potential critics, even as it began a more promising effort to reform the agrarian and general economies of Taiwan. These simultaneous campaigns of political suppression and economic reform could be considered symbolic of the political economy of Taiwan during the subsequent decades of Guomindang control.[15]

ACHIEVING STABILITY, 1949–61

Given the rough start that the regime had made in its governance of Taiwan, the Guomindang had virtually no political base in the island's constituent majority, made up of Han Chinese of Fujianese or Hakka heritage whose ancestors had lived for two or three centuries on Taiwan. The regime did have support from the mainlanders who by January were fleeing to Taiwan at the rate of 5,000 refugees per day and who would continue to make their way to Taiwan into the early 1950s, when their numbers reached about two million. At that point, the mainlander population represented about 25 percent of the roughly eight million people on Taiwan. There was a tendency on the part of the Taiwanese—that is to say the Han Chinese whose ancestors had long dwelt on the island—to lump all mainlanders together as outsiders with little stake in the life of Taiwan but with necks to save from the Communist ax. The hordes of mainlanders arriving over such an abbreviated time span greatly exacerbated an already calamitous economic situation. By the latter half of 1949, widespread crime, endemic urban unemployment, grave shortages of food and housing, and inflation that roared at an annual 3,000 percent rate characterized the economy.[16]

In such a situation, it was fortuitous for the Guomindang regime that the Korean War broke out in June 1950. Support from the Guomindang's U.S. benefactors in the Anti-Japanese War of Resistance (as the Asian-Pacific manifestation of World War II in China was called) had turned tepid with the Guomindang's miserable performance in the Chinese Civil War. For a brief moment in the late 1940s the U.S. government actually considered recognizing the People's Republic of China, formally established on October 1, 1949. Then troops doing the bidding of the communist government of North Korea invaded South Korea, and soldiers from mainland China soon joined the fray. President Harry Truman of the United States committed the Seventh Fleet to the waters of the Taiwan strait, forestalling a communist attack from the mainland. The status of Taiwan as an area free of communist control became part of the U.S. policy of containment. So recently living with the fear that his Chinese Communist Party rivals would send their forces across the strait, Guomindang leader Chiang Kai-shek could now breathe a bit more easily and begin doing what he had proved incapable of doing on the mainland: establishing the foundation for a viable and enduring government.[17]

Though Chiang had resigned the presidency of the Republic of China on the mainland as his troops withered before the communist advance, he had retained his position at the head of the Guomindang. In the spring of 1950 the Emergency Committee of the Legislative Yuan asked Chiang to resume the presidency, paving the way for his inauguration March 1, 1950. In his inaugural address he apologized for past failures and resolved to learn from his mistakes. Bolstered by U.S. reaction to events in Korea, Chiang set about reconstructing an authoritarian political party of greater integrity and competence, even as he simultaneously turned his attention to the grave economic crisis. During the years 1949–52 Chiang and his advisers achieved considerable success in reinvigorating the Guomindang. Chiang established a Central Reform Committee that temporarily absorbed the powers of the Central Executive Committee and the Central Security Council of the Guomindang. Party members were evaluated for re-registration and purged if deemed to be incompetent, corrupt, or politically threatening to Chiang and those close to him. Thirteen thousand cadres underwent re-education over the 1949–52 period. Despite the purges, Guomindang party membership tripled during the period. Nearly 6 in 10 members were of Taiwanese ethnicity, and thus the party had at last made a start on securing the political support of the Taiwanese people.[18]

Taiwan, along with the nearby islands of Penghu, Jinmen (Quemoy), and Mazu (Matsu), now represented the geographical scope of the Republic of China. Chiang and his party pledged to retake the mainland, and perhaps they were even serious about this claim during the 1950s. But as time passed, the dream faded, and the Republic of China and Taiwan formed at least a geographical identity. The fiction of being the legitimate government of mainland China remained, though, as a matter of political symbolism and as a way of securing mainlander control of the National Assembly and the Legislative Yuan. The National Assembly held constitutional authority to elect the president, authorize presidential appointments, and pass constitutional amendments. The Legislative Yuan functioned as a congress for passing laws pertinent to the ongoing life of the polity. Both of these institutions originated in the Guomindang of Sun Yat-sen on mainland China, and for two decades the membership of these two bodies was drawn from those hailing from the various provinces of the mainland. The membership at this central level of legislative power was frozen, pending that day when the Guomindang could retake the mainland and therefore hold new elections in the provinces of China. This of course conveniently excluded the Taiwanese from participation at this level of lawmaking.[19]

But another layer of island-wide legislative power was established in Taizhong, where the provincial government was located. The governor of Taiwan province was appointed by the central government, but the members of the provincial government were elected by representatives in county-level assemblies. For decades Guomindang membership was a virtual necessity for election because other political parties were effectively banned. But as a matter of demographics, the membership was guaranteed to be mostly Taiwanese, so it was in this legislative body that the island's longtime inhabitants had their highest level of legislative influence. Elections were also held at the county (*xian*) level of governance and in most cities (*shi*). For many decades, though, two cities, Taibei and Gaoxiong, were designated as special municipalities where the position of mayor was filled with central government appointees.[20]

In addition to the Legislative Yuan, there were four other main bodies of the central government structure, thus providing the five-branch adapta-

tion that Sun Yat-sen (whose writings and speeches informed the constitution of the Republic of China) made to the three-branch American system.
Similar to the American branches were an Executive Yuan, headed by the
president of the Republic of China and holding the power to execute laws;
and a Judicial Yuan, the highest court in the land with which all the lower
courts were associated. In addition, there was a Control Yuan that had a
function similar to the Censorate in the days of imperial China, responsible for investigating and evaluating the performance of officials; and there
was the Examination Yuan, also with roots in imperial China, for the
recruitment, examination, and selection of civil servants. At the highest
levels these organs were dominated by mainlanders for at least two
decades, although Taiwanese did find their way into the lower levels of
civil service.[21]

While the provincial and local elections gave a veneer of democracy to
this system, Guomindang party control was virtually complete, and the
atmosphere on the island would be that of a military dictatorship. In May
1948 the National Assembly passed the Temporary Provisions Effective
during the Period of Mobilization for Suppression of the Communist
Rebellion. Martial law was thereby reinstated, no new political parties
were allowed, and the number of newspapers was frozen at the prevailing
level of government-controlled or -dominated publications. A highly
skilled graduate of the Virginia Military Institute, Sun Liren, was tapped to
be commander in chief of the Chinese Army, which he would soon mold
into a 200,000-soldier network of highly trained and even elite troops. In
1950 President Chiang Kai-shek made his son, Chiang Ching-kuo (Jiang
Jingguo), the head of the Political Affairs Department of the Ministry of
Defense. Later the younger Chiang would also head the Academy for
Political Officers, which trained the cadres under his authority that were
responsible for propaganda among soldiers. Chiang Ching-kuo was in fact
a major power figure in all matters relevant to propaganda and security. He
headed the Chinese Anticommunist National Salvation Youth Corps,
which was the only legal association for college and university students,
and the Political Affairs Committee, charged with investigating and perse-
cuting anyone with inclinations to oppose the framework of Guomindang
rule.[22]

As the regime of Chiang Kai-shek established a tight governing apparatus on Taiwan, it also sought to make those changes necessary in the
island's economy that could provide the underpinnings of popular support.
Even to the most optimistic and die-hard advocates of the return-to-the-
mainland scenario, a clear-headed assessment yielded the conclusion that

the Guomindang and the Republic of China would be based on Taiwan for a very long time to come. Simply bludgeoning the population into acquiescence could not be a very promising way to ensure a long-term hold on power. While the theory of Sun Yat-sen featured some socialist elements of resource distribution, income equity, and limited government ownership of some means of production, there was great scope in the politico-economic system that he envisioned for private enterprise and the initiative of entrepreneurs. Similarly, the policy of the Guomindang featured a great deal of government control in major industries and cross-island infrastructure, but it also left most of the economy to the entrepreneurial energy of private citizens. The government controlled steel mills, shipbuilding facilities, cement-making factories, railroads, telecommunications firms, power companies, and sugar production operations and maintained a monopoly over the production of tobacco and alcohol. To be sure, government coffers were amply filled with the revenue that these operations provided, and well-connected individuals privy to particular profit-making opportunities associated with these and other operations made huge profits. But the approach also was driven by the logic that only the government in this still-undeveloped economy held the amount of capital necessary to bring major concerns such as these into operation quickly. More private involvement in heavy industry and the constituent elements of the island's infrastructure could come as the economy progressed. And private entrepreneurs and their hardworking labor forces would be the engines of economic progress.[23]

The government started in 1949 to make those decisions necessary to create a better overall economic climate. In June 1949 the regime introduced the New Taiwan (NT) dollar at the exchange rate of one new currency note to 40,000 old Taiwan dollars. In March 1950, preferential interest rates were established to absorb the surfeit of low-value currency floating around and undermining public confidence. For several years these rates were fixed at 7 percent per month; when compounded monthly, the rate of return came to about 125 percent per year. Only in November 1952 did this rate fall to 2 percent per month, signaling that the transition to the new currency had been successful. Success could also be read in figures indicating a rapidly falling rate of inflation. By 1950 the inflation rate was 300 percent, still high but one-tenth the rate that had prevailed at the height of the crisis in late 1949. The rate of inflation continued to fall during the next three years until landing at a very manageable level of 8 percent by 1952 and hovering near this level for the remainder of the decade. By 1953, prewar production levels had been achieved for most consumer goods, and overall production value was beginning to move above the highs achieved during the years of Japanese colonial control. Much had been done to win public confidence in the Guomindang's management of the island's economy.[24]

Over half of the labor force derived income from the agricultural economy, the expansion of which the regime was counting on to provide capital for industrial investment. Toward this end, and with the aim of winning the crucial support of Taiwan's farmers, the government listened to its American advisers and concluded that it must embark on a thoroughgoing transformation in the pattern of land ownership. It could not afford the kind of rural discontent among the farming majority that had plagued the regime during its tenure on the mainland if it hoped to build a stable society and a viable economy. Accordingly, the government superintended a land reform program that would be worthy of emulation in many parts of the globe.[25]

First came rent reduction, beginning in April 1949. Rents were fixed at 37.5 percent of the annual crop yield, a figure arrived at with solid logic and an attention to fairness for both tenants and landlords. It was determined that farmers deserved 25 percent of the annual yield as compensation for their labor and for their investments in seeds, tools, animals, and any improvements due to technological innovation. The remaining 75 percent should be split between tenant and landlord, meaning 37.5 percent in rent for the latter. This program was relatively easy to implement and brought immediate benefit to farmers, who in some regions of the island were paying 50 percent rental rates or even as much as 75 percent in areas where landlords maintained a great deal of social power and influence.[26]

Second came the program for the sale of public lands. The government held 181,490 *jia* in land, confiscated from the colonial administration and departing private Japanese interests. This was one-fifth of the arable land on Taiwan. Prices were set at two and a half times the annual yield of the main crop; the prevailing market rate was five to eight times the annual yield. Farmers could purchase a paddy field as small as one-half *jia* but no larger than two *jia*. The range of purchasable dry field was one to four *jia*. The sale of this much land with firm limits on the amount of purchasable surface area enabled a number of farmers to become owner-cultivators for the first time.[27]

Even these two significant improvements to the landholding pattern on Taiwan could not match the drastic change wrought by the third and most radical plank of the Guomindang's land reform program, which operated on the principle of land-to-the-tiller. According to this program, landlords were forced to give up all of their land beyond a limit of three *jia* of medium-grade paddy field or six *jia* of dry field. A lengthy table of equivalencies was established to account for different levels of land quality, so that landlords holding premium-grade land would keep less than the medium-grade limit while landlords owning poorer-grade land would keep more. But whatever the particular limit for a given landlord, the transfers to those doing the actual tilling of the soil were considerable, and it was this plank of the land reform program that was most responsible for transforming the pattern of land tenure in rural Taiwan. For many landlords the program was of course cause for substantial consternation, but they did not go away empty-handed. They were compensated at two and a half times the annual yield, the same arrangement that prevailed in the government land sales program. Since the market rate was two to three times that, the landlords did sustain substantial losses to the benefit of the tillers. The compensation came in the form of land bonds and stock holdings in four major government corporations, with land bonds representing 70 percent of the compensation and stock holdings making up 30 percent. Many landlords eventually chose to sell these bonds to more entrepreneurial or financier types, but some of the rural elite began to look to the industrial and commercial sectors of the economy and to make a successful reorientation in their personal and family economies.[28]

Together, the planks of the land reform program created an owner-cultivator–dominated rural scene. By the end of 1953, 139,267 hectares had been transferred to 194,823 families that had formerly been tenants. Only 36 percent of farm families in 1949 had been owner-cultivators, but by 1952 65 percent of farm families tilled their own land. Highly motivated to produce more on land that they cultivated to the exclusive benefit of themselves and their families, they found that yields and income rose dramatically. The farm family's average income rose 81 percent between 1949 and 1952, and in the latter year rice yields surpassed prewar levels. Avoiding the temptation to rush toward industrialization and showy urban projects that characterize so many cases of third-world development, the Guomindang regime and their American advisers gave a great deal of time and attention to the matter of agricultural development. Advised by a Sino-American organization known as the Joint Commission on Rural Reconstruction, the government established farmers' associations in township centers throughout the island; these associations provided virtually all farmers with adequate services in matters of rural credit and savings, sales and marketing, health and sanitation, and transportation. The farmers' associations also marketed government-produced fertilizer, for which farmers had to barter with a portion of their rice yields. The terms of this exchange greatly favored the government, which simultaneously obtained rice reserves for price stabilization and gained funds for projects in the industrial sector and investments in infrastructure.[29]

The United States looked the other way as the regime it supported engaged in brutal suppression of anything that smacked of political dissent or the assertion of rights on the part of the Taiwanese people against the so recently arrived mainlanders who now held governing authority. The United States, knee-deep in the trenches of the Cold War, sought a show-case for capitalist development. Accordingly, the U.S. Congress authorized the founding of the U.S. Military Assistance and Advisory Group and from 1951 to 1965 funneled $1.5 million of nonmilitary aid toward the devel-opment of the Taiwanese economy. Through such organizations as the Joint Commission on Rural Reconstruction and the U.S. Military Assis-tance and Advisory Group, American advisers were in a position to keep tabs on the assistance provided and exert pressure with regard to its allo-cation. The Guomindang regime poured two-thirds of the money into investment in infrastructure.[30]

By 1954 the United States was encouraged enough by the reform pro-gram of the Guomindang to sign the Taiwan–United States Mutual Defense Treaty, so that the great benefactor of the Chiang Kai-shek regime was now investing heavily in both the economic development and the mil-itary defense capability of Taiwan. For two decades the United States would continue to support the convenient fiction that the Republic of China legitimately included the mainland, even if in the minor matter of actual control the real possibility of this faded with each passing year. Astonishingly, the government on Taiwan was able to sustain its seat in the United Nations until 1971 as the sole representative of a China that was actually governed by the communists to whom Chiang and his armies had lost the civil war. By no means did the tensions between Taiwanese and mainlanders ever abate during the years of rapid economic development and international recognition. But most Taiwanese signed on to a tempo-rary deal. Desiring to keep their lives in the face of Chiang Ching-kuo's efficient security apparatus, and elated at the improvement of their eco-nomic standard of living, most of the island's hardworking people concen-trated on the continuing improvement of their family economies and put their political aspirations on hold. In the course of time, some people were encouraged that the United States was giving their island so much support and hoped that eventually the Guomindang would activate the more dem-ocratic aspects of the Three Principles of the People studied by all public school, college, and university students and widely touted as the prescription for China's ills.[31]

So it became imperative to the Guomindang that its economic program succeed. This was the heart of the deal it was cutting with the Taiwanese people: The Guomindang and the mainlanders would for the foreseeable future keep political authority, and the Taiwanese would see dramatic improvement in their economic lives. In the task of economic construction, the Guomindang could draw upon the expertise of a considerable number of well-educated and, in many cases, U.S.-trained professionals, who had been frustrated with the regime's incompetent showing on the mainland but who were given greater rein to implement thoughtful programs in the new political context. Two of the most important were Yin Zhongyong (K. Y. Yin) and Li Guoding (K. T. Li). Yin was trained in the United States as an electrical engineer; Li, who also earned an advanced degree in the United States, was a physicist. But these two took their technical expertise and rationalist mindset into their study of the Taiwanese economy. In a well-conceived progression through successful stages and artful shifts of policy at just the right time, advisers such as these nudged the Guomindang into a number of fortuitous decisions that would make the island's economic development a wonder of the developing world.[32]

During the 1950s the Guomindang government elected for a program of import substitution. Such a program endeavors to protect infant industries and to secure a dependable domestic market for the goods that those industries produce. The United States was solidly behind this program, offering an abundance of assistance and advice along the way. In 1951, at the urging of advisers at the U.S. Agency for International Development, the Guomindang government established the Economic Stabilization Board to serve as the key organ for making economic policy. This governmental body and its later incarnations devised a series of four-year economic plans that transformed the Taiwanese economy. The first plan that the board devised and implemented, the Four-Year Economic Plan for 1953–56, called for particular emphasis on the protection of industries generating electricity, fertilizers, and textiles; of these, textiles gained the most attention of policymakers. The government furnished industrial entrepreneurs willing to erect factories for textile production with start-up capital and raw cotton imported at bargain prices from the United States. In support of textile manufacturing and other industries identified for protection and support under the import substitution scheme, the administration instituted a number of policies that provided the domestic environment in which the favored industries could flourish. The regime set a high nominal tariff rate of 44.7 percent; and on some items that the government was particularly keen to protect, the rate rose as high as 160 percent. Also in support of the import substitution principle, the administration established a unified exchange rate that made the New Taiwan dollar relatively weak in comparison to the U.S. dollar, thus making domestic goods cheap in comparison to foreign goods. In 1955 the exchange rate was revised so as to raise the number of New Taiwan dollars needed to acquire one U.S. dollar from NT$15.55 to NT$25. That number went up again to NT$35 in 1958, and then in 1960 it shot up once more to NT$40.[33]

In 1957–60 the second four-year economic plan, which included greater focus on matters of employment and income, went into effect. While continuing the first plan's emphasis on development of light industry, this second plan shifted some of the focus to heavy industry, particularly that which contributed to national defense. A great deal of capital flowed into the four industries in which landlords had been issued stocks. Accordingly, Taiwan Cement, Taiwan Pulp and Paper, Taiwan Industry and Mining, and Taiwan Agriculture and Forestry thrived. Many landlords chose to sell their stock holdings to more aggressive, experienced investors, and many of those purchasing the stocks made huge profits on investments in cement, petrochemicals, plastics, and processed agricultural goods.[34]

A number of indicators from the 1953–60 period demonstrate considerable success for the government's import substitution policy. The industrial production index rose 154.7 percent during these years, and income per person went up 40 percent. The Taiwan Electric Company realized a 150 percent expansion of electric power capacity. Textiles and other favored industries were thriving on low production costs and cheap labor, which at this stage the regime saw as a substitute for expensive machinery. The strategy here was to absorb excess rural and urban labor, bolster employment, stabilize family economies, strengthen the domestic market, and exercise patience in considering more generous outlays for capital inputs that could reduce profits and take jobs away.[35]

By the late 1950s there were signs that the benefits of the import substitution policy had run their course. The domestic market was saturated. Clothing and other consumer goods were plentiful but showed little potential for market expansion in a strictly domestic-market context. Although urban jobs had greatly increased and rural industrialization had brought some additional employment opportunity to the countryside, a great deal of underemployment of rural labor still existed, thus extending the potential for additional cheap labor if only the number of enterprises capable of tapping it could be increased. This oversupply of inexpensive labor was only underscored by a population growth rate that stood at the typically high rate of 3.6 percent for a developing country. The population had grown to ten million by 1958, up two million from the figure at the beginning of the decade. The economy, having made great progress in the course of the 1950s, was still dominated by agriculture, which in 1958 provided 86 percent of all exports and employed 52 percent of the labor force. If Taiwan was to project itself into the modern world as the showcase for economic development that the United States hoped it would be, industry would have to play a greater role and import substitution should give way to a more export-oriented strategy. So, with the courage and foresight that would come to be the hallmark of Guomindang economic policy, Taiwan's policymakers shifted gears and engineered a new export-based strategy to achieve the goal of developing the island's economy.[36]

TRIUMPHS AND CHALLENGES, 1962–79

At the very end of the 1950s and into the early 1960s, the Guomindang administration made a number of adjustments that it and its American advisers considered necessary to the achievement of a more mature and export-oriented economy. Foreign exchange controls were liberalized, the number of goods designated for protection was reduced, more banks were brought into operation to serve the credit needs of entrepreneurs, and a stock market was established to give businesspersons the option of seeking investment from the broad and now more prosperous population. In September 1960 the Legislative Yuan passed the Statute for the Encouragement of Investment for Industrial Construction, signaling the government's great willingness to create a very attractive climate for foreign investment in the industries of Taiwan. By the provisions of this statute, firms showing an appropriate plan and inclination to produce for the export market would benefit from a five-year tax holiday. The business tax was set at a maximum of 18 percent. Imports of foreign machinery that would be used to churn out goods for export would now come with a tax exemption. Likewise, a tax exemption was applicable to imported raw materials used in the manufacture of goods for the international market. The government also offered assistance to entrepreneurs looking to market their goods abroad, essentially helping these entrepreneurs to find affordable land on which to establish their factories and offices. The Central Bank of China was reactivated in 1961 with the charge to stabilize the currency, promote production, and assist in economic development. Two other banks were chartered: the Bank of China, which became known for assisting domestic industries and enterprises with funds and advice to support the vision of growth through expansion of exports; and the Bank of Communications, the special function of which was to deal with issues of foreign exchange and international trade. A third four-year economic plan to cover the years 1961–64 came with the stated chief goal of "accelerating economic development" through an export orientation. The labor-intensive strategy of investment was to be continued and expanded, with particular emphasis on textiles, plastics, rubber, paper and paper products, and chemicals.[37]

Taiwan's labor force was itself an inducement to foreign countries to establish their factories on the island. A foreign firm that perceived the labor force in its own country as having become too expensive, or as lacking in motivation and productivity commensurate with wages paid, could well see Taiwan as a haven where low-priced, hardworking labor was in abundant supply.

Hard work for the economic betterment of their families was for most Taiwanese a religious imperative. Prospering economically allowed them to offer more elaborate sacrifices to their ancestors and thus to provide them a better standard of living in the material components of the afterlife. Working long hours allowed them to accumulate enough money to upgrade the family diet, to acquire a few modern conveniences, and to provide their children with the best possible education and start-up capital when they embarked on careers that would in turn do honor to the family and bolster its financial reserves. But in the frugal mindset of the Taiwanese, the ultimate goal was to save and invest and make the family economy grow so that generations to come would prosper. In all of this the idea was to serve all links in the family chain—those who had come before, those presently living, and those yet to come. The ancestors of the Taiwanese had for the most part come from Fujian or Guangdong looking for the opportunity to strengthen this chain, to get themselves in a situation to provide a better life for this family broadly construed. On the Taiwan frontier, these hardy pioneers had toiled and moved and toiled and moved on again to get to a place where land was plentiful and their fortunes could be staked. Some got to places that were so remote or where the realities of local control were so to their favor that they could avoid huge exactions from those who wanted to claim the better part of their surplus production. But for centuries, the Dutch, then the Zheng family, then the landlords who grew powerful under Qing rule, then the Japanese and the local elite that the colonialists favored, stood ready to claim as much of that surplus as they could. The ability of noncultivators to claim that surplus reached unprecedented heights under the Japanese regime.[38]

So when the Guomindang regime implemented land reform, Taiwan's farmers took every opportunity to acquire their own land and engage in increasingly productive agricultural labor. As factories sprouted up, they seized the chance to send the surplus labor from their families out to the rural industrial parks or the export-processing zones or the cities so as to maximize the family income-earning capacity. And their children received better education with each passing year. Between 1952 and 1960, the number of primary schools grew from 1,248 to 1,982; the number of secondary schools doubled from 148 to 299; and post-secondary schools tripled in number, from just 4 to 15. In 1952, just 58 percent of the island's children attended school—a drop from levels achieved late in the Japanese administration. By 1960, the figure stood at 73 percent, close to the high point of the Japanese era. In the course of the 1960s that figure would rise still further, to 85 percent by 1970. During the years 1954–68, the Guomindang government poured 13 percent of its total budget into education and by the latter year had increased the number of years of compulsory schooling from six to nine years. Accordingly, the percentage of those going on to junior high after primary school increased from 51 percent in 1961 to 80 percent in 1971. Not surprisingly, foreign countries found on Taiwan a valuable resource: a well-educated, highly motivated work force that perceived unprecedented opportunity to provide a better life for all of those along the family continuum. Furthermore, a work force under this psychology of perceived opportunity was not likely to turn rebellious; and with an authoritarian regime ready to strike down any effort at meaningful labor organization, the chance of this sort of trouble for foreign management was virtually nonexistent. Domestic and foreign investors and industrialists alike eagerly flocked to Taiwan to take advantage of the government inducements and the high-quality, passive labor force.[39]

Three export-processing zones were established between 1966 and 1968. These offered the best possible terms and conditions to foreign investors: cheap land, abundant power, quality labor, and low taxes. By 1968 domestic and foreign investment in the first zone near Gaoxiong had reached US$1.8 million, export value averaged US$7.2 million annually, and the labor force had grown to 1,500. Two other zones, a second one near Gaoxiong and one near Taizhong, proved to be similarly successful. But the genius of the Taiwan case of development is that it wasn't concentrated in these zones, or in a single city, or even in a handful of cities. All around the island industrial parks were established in rural areas, providing nearby economic opportunities for expendable agricultural labor. The largest cities themselves were dispersed—Taibei to the northwest, Jilong to the northeast, Tainan to the southwest, Gaoxiong to the far south, and Taizhong near the midpoint along the western coast. And everywhere in Taiwan were smaller cities and vital township centers whose residents eagerly set up small-scale workshops and tiny factories employing a hand-ful of workers, taking their place in a chain of production that led up to the larger factories and on to the great international marketplace.[40]

The results were astonishing, giving rise to a characterization so oft-used that it now seems trite: the "Taiwan miracle." Between 1960 and 1970, export value increased eightfold, from US$174 million to US$1.56 billion. Imports grew from US$252 million to US$1.52 billion. During that decade, average annual growth of the gross national product was 9.7 percent; the growth rate of per capita income was 6.6 percent. Whereas in 1953 income distribution in Taiwan was much like that in Mexico or Brazil, with a wide gap between the poorest and the wealthiest citizens, by 1970 Taiwan's distribution of income was among the world's most equi-table, better than that of the United States. As per capita income went up, and with the gains so evenly distributed, domestic investment from domestic savings grew from 60 percent in 1960 to 95 percent in 1970. With all of this growth and prosperity had come a dramatic structural transformation of the economy. A labor force that had been 52.1 percent agrarian in 1952 and only 20.2 percent industrial had shifted by 1970 to create a rather even distribution: 35 percent agrarian, 30 percent industrial, and the remaining 35 percent commercial or service. The growth rate in the industrial sector for 1953–70 was 14.2 percent; growth occurred in the agricultural sector, too, but at a more humble 4.9 percent rate.[41]

Taiwan's contemporary history reveals the abiding irony that the more economically successful and culturally developed the society has become, the more insecure its diplomatic status. Throughout the 1950s and 1960s, as the island's industrious people were working hard to achieve economic success in the context of an essentially capitalist economy governed by harsh military dictatorship, the United States threw its considerable pres-tige behind the Republic of China in its pretense to represent the people of the mainland, and Taiwan as a mere province. But as the island entered the 1970s with an immensely more developed economy, as some people on the island and many across the world grew contemptuous of the Chiang regime's claim on mainland China, and as a few brave voices on Taiwan ventured to register dissent, the United States signaled that its formal diplomatic recognition of the regime was on the wane.

At times in the 1960s it had seemed that the United States and the People's Republic of China might come to blows over Vietnam, so that it suited the purpose of Chiang's great benefactor to continue its diplomatic recognition and to avail itself of the Ching Chuan Kang Airfield on Taiwan for transporting, refueling, and airlifting supplies destined for Vietnam. Thousands of U.S. servicemen doing tours of duty in Vietnam took rest and relaxation (R & R) leave on the island. Taiwan continued to be an important link in the United States' wall of containment. But in the course of the 1960s, the rift between the People's Republic of China and its fellow communist colossus, the Soviet Union, widened. Even as the People's Republic became a nuclear power, the great communist theorist and towering leader Mao Zedong looked across the Pacific to the leader of world capitalism for diplomatic leverage. For their part, President Richard Nixon of the United States and his foreign policy adviser–cum–secretary of state, Henry Kissinger, saw in the People's Republic of China a so-called "China card" that might be useful in their contest for world influence against the Soviet Union.[42]

The first strong indication that the diplomatic universe of the United States and Taiwan had been dramatically altered came in 1971. The United States let it be known that it would not object if the United Nations voted recognition to the People's Republic of China, and the General Assembly of the international gathering of nations did so. Then in July 1971 Kissinger traveled to China for a rendezvous with Mao and Premier Zhou Enlai, paving the way for Nixon's own journey to his old Cold War nemesis in February 1972. At the end of that landmark visit, Nixon and the Chinese leadership jointly issued the Shanghai Communique, agreeing that there was but one China and that the issue of who represented the nation should be resolved peacefully. The "one China" policy continued to prevail into the 1990s and to serve even in the year 2000 as the agreement against which other views had to contend. By January 1979 the administration of President Jimmy Carter made it clear that the United States saw the People's Republic as having the strongest claim to be the legitimate government for the greater body of Chinese people; for the first time, the United States broke off formal diplomatic relations with the Republic of China on Taiwan and gave that recognition to the communist rulers of the mainland.[43]

During the 1970s the Guomindang faced its greatest test of legitimacy since the early days of the party's rule on the island. The years 1971–73 were particularly trying. Soon after the government lost its seat in the United Nations, the government of Japan shifted its recognition to the

People's Republic of China. Then in 1973 came the Six-Day Yom Kippur War that precipitated an international oil crisis. Taiwan's economy was so dependent on foreign oil that the turbulence was bound to have an impact on the island's industries. The inflation rate during the mid-1970s was the highest that the economy of Taiwan had seen since the early days of Guomindang rule. High prices came as a blow to both urban and rural residents after two decades of moderate inflation and greatly expanding income. Farmers had already been complaining since the late 1960s that conditions in the agricultural sector were deteriorating due to such problems as declining farm size, decreasing competitiveness of their crops on the international marketplace, politicized and less efficacious farmers' associations, and a system of marketing that seemed designed to benefit middlepersons more than the tillers of the soil. Urban workers complained, too, that their wages were not keeping pace with rising consumer prices. The Guomindang was attentive enough to farmers' complaints to end the major resource extraction devices that had generated so much capital for investment in infrastructure and industrial expansion: In 1973 the rice-fertilizer barter system was discontinued, and the terms of compulsory rice purchases were changed so as to transform this exchange from a government income earner into an effective subsidy to farmers.[44]

Meanwhile, the government worked hard to maintain acceptable foreign relationships in the changed context of the 1970s. After breaking off formal relations with the government that called itself the Republic of China, the government of Japan established a quasi-official agency on Taiwan to perform the same essential functions that its embassy had exercised before official ties were severed. The blow to international prestige that the Chiang regime sustained as Japan withdrew formal recognition was very real, but in practical terms interaction between Japan and Taiwan went on much as before. The United States followed the Japanese example after its own break with the Republic of China in 1979, establishing the American Institute in Taiwan (AIT) to carry on business with the island and implement joint agreements much as before. Other nations followed suit, striving as did Japan and the United States to have it both ways: conducting diplomatic relations with the government that ruled the world's most populous nation without entirely severing economic ties with the government that presided over one of the world's most dynamic economies.[45]

And despite the oil shocks of 1973–74, the Taiwanese economy continued to advance. The transformation from an agrarian-led to an industry-led economy became even more pronounced: By 1980 agriculture's share of the labor force in Taiwan had fallen to 20 percent; industry claimed 42 percent, while service and commerce employed 38 percent of the work force. Likewise, exports were more important than ever, contributing 80 percent of manufacturing growth during 1971–76. Exports during the decade ending in 1980 increased 789 percent. All of this industrial expansion, however, severely strained the infrastructure that the government had worked so hard to build. Despite continued expansion of power facilities, growth in demand for electricity outstripped the rate of increase in power generation. By the late 1970s, the Guomindang regime made one of those artful policy decisions that made its management of the Taiwanese economy a case of sustained success. During the late 1970s, the regime implemented its plan for Ten Major Projects, pouring US$8 billion into a variety of projects intended to upgrade the infrastructure to suit the needs of an economy that was rapidly approaching industrialized status. Included in this package of projects was a new north-south superhighway, a fully modern international airport, two new port facilities, an improved railway system, a second nuclear reactor, and expanded industrial capacity at the government's steel mill and shipbuilding facilities. Then, even before all of these projects were completed, the government upped expenditures another US$23 billion and invested in 14 additional projects. By the end of the 1970s, the government had doubled the length of its highways, tripled its supply of electricity, modernized and expanded its rail and air transport systems, increased its ability to handle foreign ships calling at its ports, and in many ways abetted the growth of industry and trade.[46]

The person at the helm as Taiwan navigated its way into newly industrialized status was Chiang Ching-kuo, who had become premier in 1971 and then assumed the presidency when his father died in 1975. Chiang Ching-kuo's career stands as something of a metaphor for the political development of Taiwan as a whole. Widely respected for his personal integrity and administrative ability, the younger Chiang had made his mark as a party reformer and tough, even ruthless, head of the state security network. His work in the latter capacity became ever tougher, as slowly but surely in this fast-developing society there emerged a brave few who boldly made the first forays into political protest since the February 28th Incident. The leading pioneer of the kind of protest that would press more and more firmly on the doors of acceptability in the late 1970s was Peng Mingmin, who in the 1960s served as chair of the Political Science Department at National Taiwan University. Peng and his students Xie Congmin and Wei Tingchao issued a document called the "Self-Rescue Declaration of Taiwan." Espousing the view that Taiwan had already achieved de facto independence, they asserted that there was no excuse for delaying the implementation of democracy, one of Sun Yat-sen's Three Principles of the People. This brave claim that Taiwan was an independent country, however true by one system of logic, was totally unacceptable in the authoritarian climate of the 1960s. Their assertions earned Peng and his students long prison terms. Peng enjoyed great respect among international human rights advocates, who pressured the United States to press the Guomindang for Peng's release. He was granted amnesty in November 1964 and, after several years of frustration in a constant yet lower-key push for greater political freedom, departed for self-imposed exile in Sweden in 1970.[47]

Sheer reality was catching up to the Guomindang, though, in its claim to be the representative of all China. The representatives of the mainland provinces no longer controlled by the Guomindang began to die, thinning the membership of both the National Assembly and the Legislative Yuan. From 1969 forward the government periodically held elections to supplement the memberships of the two legislatures. Thus in the chief lawmaking bodies there began the slow but steady process of Taiwanization that also took place in some posts at the upper echelons of the government and the military. After he assumed the presidency in 1975, Chiang Ching-kuo accelerated the process of Taiwanization of the party and government, recognizing that the party and its government needed two things to survive: They had to have fresh talent, and they had to have a greater foundation of support in this rapidly modernizing society than that which had been built with a strong economy.[48]

Economic success had enabled the Taiwanese people to buy more than consumer goods and a higher standard of living. It also bought more time to consider other realms of life beyond the material. Cultural endeavors had been given short shrift in the rush to development, but such matters gained greater attention in this increasingly middle-class society as the 1970s came to a close. In the realm of literature there raged what was known as the Nativist Literary Debate *(xiangtu wenxue lunzhan)*. Advocates of a nativist literature launched virulent criticisms of the modernists who had dominated the world of literature on Taiwan from the 1960s. Nativists saw modernist literature as hopelessly slavish to Western forms and divorced from the reality of life on Taiwan. They called for works rendered in the Taiwanese dialect, a greater focus on the life of country folk and small-town residents, and the realistic portrayal of existence under what many clearly saw as just another imperialist regime. A number of older writers tended to favor the nativist side of the literary debate, whereas government newspapers invited articles in defense of the modernists. By mid-1978 the government had had enough of the nativists and their mostly implicit criticisms, moving to shut down publications that had given the nativist works and the stormy debate too much space.[49]

But some moved beyond literary and mostly allusive criticism onto the path that had been blazed by Peng Mingmin. By the latter half of the 1970s, a coterie of brave souls met and wrote and even occasionally took to the streets to push the cause of greater democracy on the island that they loved. In the course of the middle to late 1970s those who opposed the Guomindang and sought the right to contest the party in local and provincial elections came together under a label appropriate to those doing party-like organizing in a one-party state: *dangwai,* meaning "outside the party." Despite political persecution and the Guomindang's incessant efforts to intimidate those who challenged the ruling party for leadership in city, township, county, and provincial governments, the members of the *dangwai* movement persevered. From 1977 to 1979 *dangwai* candidates won 21 of 77 seats in provincial elections that were supposed to be a mere democratic facade justifying one of the Guomindang's convenient fictions, the image it tried to project as "Free China." The *dangwai* also won 4 out of 20 elections for the head position in cities, townships, and counties. When citizens took to the streets of Zhongli in protest over voting irregularities that represented an apparent Guomindang attempt to stem this tide of successful challenges to its rule, there occurred one of many serious clashes that would take place in this previously rather quiescent post-1949 society. Police and demonstrators clashed, the police station was stormed and burned, and casualties accumulated on both sides. Many Taiwanese still looking literally just to go about their business, to maintain the prosperity that had enabled them to more bountifully fulfill their religious obligations to the family than at any other time in Taiwanese history, proved susceptible to government condemnations of demonstrators as disturbers of the public order. Stability *(anding)* is a high value among Taiwanese and Chinese societies everywhere, and the desire for it among this island's populace would buy the Guomindang several more years to work out a new sociopolitical scheme that the more prescient saw as inevitable. But the *dangwai* continued to do its job of opening eyes to a world beyond prosperity to an existence in which democracy and nationhood held a role.[50]

On December 10, 1979, *dangwai* members gathered with leaders Shi Mingde and Lu Xiulian for a march on the streets of Gaoxiong. The movement's chief journal, *Meili dao* ("Beautiful Island," after the Portuguese *Ilha Formosa*), had been full of reports related to the event. On December 9, 1979, one of the staff members at *Meili dao* headquarters had been the victim of a clandestine attack, a warning that Shi, Lu, and company ignored. They took to the streets of Gaoxiong, the island's hotbed of antigovernment thought and organization. Some of the less circumspect marchers hurled provocative statements at police officers, who had been given the directive to keep a tight rein on the demonstrators. Police brought out the tear gas. *Dangwai* leaders yelled out through microphones on the trucks they rode. They urged everyone to stay calm, continue to march, deliver their message, and yet remain peaceful. But the demonstrators lost their cool. Taunts between the marchers and the police escalated, and the participants eventually dispersed in confusion. Leaders of the march rode to Tainan and reassembled at the Tainan Hotel. But law enforcement officials soon had leader Lu Xiulian and fellow activists Yao Jiawen, Zhang Zhunhong, Lin Yixiong, Lin Hongxuan, and Chen Zhu under arrest. Shi Mingde managed to slip out of Tainan and stay on the run for several months. His wife, American scholar Linda Gail Arrigo, was deported.[51]

The Guomindang dug in. During the first half of the 1980s life on the surface in Taiwan went on much as before. But in the underground of democracy advocates and independence enthusiasts, the dream of a different kind of Taiwan became more and more real with each passing year. Chiang Ching-kuo, ultimately a perspicacious pragmatist, would begin to work out a new deal with the Taiwanese people that he hoped would satisfy increasing demands for democratization and Taiwanization while still allowing the Guomindang to maintain its leading role in the government. His efforts, together with the sheer audacity of *dangwai* activists who would not be denied, laid the groundwork for a political miracle on Taiwan in the 1980s and 1990s every bit as spectacular as the economic miracle of the previous decades.[52]

DEMOCRATIZATION AND THE QUEST FOR IDENTITY, 1980–2000

By 1980, President Chiang Ching-kuo realized that substantial changes would have to be made in the sociopolitical climate on Taiwan. The very legitimacy of his government was at stake. His father's structure of power had stood firm during the 1950s and 1960s. The Taiwanese people had during those years accepted the deal that the Guomindang had offered. Farmers, factory workers, and businesspeople all benefited from the spectacular growth that had made the Taiwanese economy an international wonder. But farmers were not so happy with their condition in the 1970s; most of their crops had lost their profitability on the international marketplace, and they were more and more dependent on off-farm income to sustain the standard of living that they had come to expect. Laborers grew restive, too, demanding a greater share of company profits, better working conditions, and benefits such as health and life insurance. The society had matured to the point that a brave vanguard of women was giving voice to feminist causes. The Presbyterian Church on Taiwan, long an advocate for better treatment of the aborigines and for the rights of the Taiwanese people, moved ever more aggressively into the realm of politics, throwing its support behind the *dangwai* movement.[53]

Chiang's most notable response at the very beginning of the 1980s was a reversion to repression. Leaders of the Gaoxiong uprising were sentenced to long prison terms. Shi Mingde was given a life sentence, while Lu Xiulian received a 12-year prison term. Gao Zhimin, secretary general of the Presbyterian Church on Taiwan, also earned a long term in prison for harboring Shi and abetting his opposition politics. But even as he came down hard on the party and the state's most visible and vocal critics, Chiang Ching-kuo moved rapidly to secure a more solid base of support among the Taiwanese people than his father's authoritarian structure could allow. Efforts were made to recruit more intellectuals into the party and to offer party-sponsored social services down to the village and township levels. An early signal that a liberalizing trend might be in the offing was given when the government legalized the syncretistic religious organization Yiguandao at mid-decade. Then in March 1986 Chiang appointed an ad hoc committee to recommend measures consistent with an appropriate level of democratization at this stage in the island's development. The committee was to study the existing framework of martial law and to recommend any changes that members thought beneficial, especially in four particular areas: (1) the ban on opposition political parties, (2) reorganization of the National Assembly and the Legislative Yuan, (3) further Taiwanization of the government and party, and (4) any reform needed in the structure and program of the Guomindang.[54]

It was a time of transition and many, many mixed signals. During the summer of 1986 opposition leader Lin Zhengjie and Taibei City Council member Chen Shuibian went to jail for advocating independence and engaging in premature political organization. This brought forth objections from many quarters, highlighting the growing impatience and intense frustration of a middle class eager to move to the next level of freedom, from the economic to the political. On September 28, the day when the Republic of China celebrates the birthday of the great sage Confucius, and well before any recommendations had emanated from the ad hoc committee studying reform issues, 135 members of the *dangwai* announced the formation of a new political party: the Democratic Progressive Party *(Minjindang)*. Soon Chiang was urging the Central Standing Committee of the Guomindang to respond positively to the demands of an increasingly restive populace. On October 15, 1986, the committee indicated that it, too, had heard the middle-class message and seen enough of its manifestations. The committee made one of the most momentous decisions in Taiwan's history under Guomindang rule, a major concession that would forever change the relationship of the party over those whom it sought to rule: It announced the government's intention to lift martial law by summer 1987; appended to this decision were measures relaxing the ban on organizing opposition parties and specifically legalizing the Democratic Progressive Party.[55]

The Democratic Progressive Party wasted no time thrusting itself into the thick of Taiwanese politics. On December 6, 1986, the first legal two-party elections were held, for open seats in the Legislative Yuan. The new party fielded 44 candidates for 73 available seats, winning 12 of them. Democratic Progressive Party candidates did well in the Taibei, Tainan, and Gaoxiong areas, a fact of great significance. More news of liberalization followed. A new National Security Act promised to make life considerably less draconian for the regime's political opponents. Unlimited conversion of the New Taiwan dollar into foreign currency was now possible. Restrictions on travel to the People's Republic of China were lifted. The nullification of martial law went into effect in July 1987. By the time a frail Chiang Ching-kuo died the following January, he could go to his rest among the ancestors knowing that he had artfully negotiated the twists and turns leading to democracy, doing so while still giving his party a chance to win the genuine support of much of the populace as it faced the challenge of redefining itself in a new era of open political contention.[56]

Chiang also left behind him an economy that had made favorable adjustments to the demands of an increasingly politicized and well-educated society. After the oil shocks of the 1970s, government economic development policy came to focus on certain "strategic industries" that required low energy consumption, technological intensity, and high value added. Particular emphasis was given to machine tools, transportation equipment, electronics, and computer information. Taiwan was destined during the 1980s and 1990s to become a world leader in the latter industry. Toward more efficient concentration of the money and talent that it took to produce such sophisticated goods, the government established Xinzhu Science-

Based Industrial Park, where 113 high-tech firms with revenues totaling NT$60 billion per annum established themselves in the 1980s alongside research and development facilities that were among the most advanced in East Asia. During 1984–88 the export value of Taiwan-manufactured computer hardware products increased fivefold, from US$1 billion to US$5.15 billion. Computers and computer peripherals made in Taiwan were recognized throughout the world for their high quality and dependability. During these years, integrated circuits, telecommunication equipment, environmental biotechnology devices, automobile equipment, and energy goods were also made and exported in large quantities.[57]

Export markets and other facets of Taiwan's economy underwent changes during the 1980s equal to those unfolding in the political arena. Impelled by growing concern in the United States over Taiwan's enormous trade surplus with the superpower, the U.S. government forced an appreciation of the New Taiwan dollar and ended Taiwan's most-favored nation status. In accord with U.S. concern, the changes in Taiwan's diplomatic status, and the desire to prove Taiwan's ability to compete in other export markets, companies took their government's cue and began to seek a variety of destinations for their goods. Whereas in 1985, 48 percent of all goods exported from Taiwan went to the United States, by the 1990s the U.S. market absorbed only 30 percent of these goods. Greater shares went especially to Hong Kong, Southeast Asia, and Western Europe, while Japan remained a major market for Taiwanese export goods.[58]

Presiding over Taiwan's transition to a mature industrial and even postindustrial economy from the late 1980s into the 1990s was one of the most gifted leaders of the late twentieth century, a man who had made his own professional transition: Lee Teng-hui. Lee's professional life began as an agricultural economist; with two advanced degrees from the United States, including a doctorate earned in 1968 from Cornell University, Lee had had a distinguished career as a professor at National Taiwan University and official at the Joint Commission on Rural Reconstruction before he ventured into the world of politics. In the late 1970s he was among those talented Taiwanese whom Chiang Ching-kuo recruited to serve in high positions in the increasingly Taiwanized Guomindang party and government. He began a steep and steady rise in his new career with a stint as appointed mayor of Taibei during 1978–81. From 1981 to 1984 he served as governor of Taiwan province, after which he was tapped by Chiang Ching-kuo to be vice president of the Republic of China in 1984. With this highly symbolic move, the increasingly frail Chiang put Lee, born in Sanchi Village near Danshui in 1923, in line to bring ethnic Taiwanese leadership to the very height of the island's government. When he took over as president upon Chiang's death in 1988, the symbol of his political position became a matter of even greater substance. Here, at last, was a true Taiwanese leader of the majority Taiwanese people of the de facto nation of Taiwan. Immediately articulating his key themes of "liberalization, democratization, and internationalization," Lee commenced a masterful transition to a fully democratized political system.[59]

The foundation for the new order was laid in a remarkable period encompassing the first two years of Lee Teng-hui's tenure as president. In July 1988 the Guomindang Party Congress overwhelmingly voted to formalize Lee's position as party leader. Furthermore, 16 of the 31 party members chosen to serve on the party's Central Committee were of Taiwanese ethnicity, the first time that a majority of ethnic Taiwanese had lent its leadership to this top party committee. The group as a whole had more representation from labor and women and was younger and more sympathetic to the cause of reform than any previous composition of the Central Committee. Lee chose to retain a mainlander, Yu Guohua, in the position he was already occupying as premier of the Republic of China, but the president maneuvered to install many reform-minded ethnic Taiwanese in key cabinet positions under the premier's formal authority. Fourteen of those appointed held doctorates from the United States. The highly sensitive and extraordinarily important position of foreign minister went to an ethnic Taiwanese. The most dramatic appointment was made to the position of finance minister: It went to Shirley Kuo, a female party member of Taiwanese ethnicity whose very presence in the cabinet broadcast that a new day was at hand in the polity of Taiwan.[60]

In December 1989 fully multiparty elections were held for positions in the Legislative Yuan, Provincial Assembly, mayoralties, counties, and city councils throughout the island. The Democratic Progressive Party did very well, winning 27 of 101 contested seats in the Legislative Yuan, numerous city council and Provincial Assembly positions, and 7 of 21 county magistrate positions, including that of Taibei *xian.* The 70 percent turnout gave strong testimony to the electorate's enthusiasm for exercising its political choices in the new atmosphere of open competition. For Lee Teng-hui and the Guomindang, this late-1989 election was a wake-up call, and the president was ready to rise and shine: Having already positioned himself and his party to make significant reforms in the political processes of the Republic of China, wanting to transform his traditionally rightist party into a more moderate exponent of change with stability, Lee seized upon the results of the elections to further advance his reformist agenda.[61]

Events in March 1990 that seemingly put Lee on the spot in actuality even better positioned Lee Teng-hui to overhaul the political system on Taiwan. From March 16 to 22, 1990, students from National Taiwan University and other universities gathered on the steps of the National Concert Hall and National Theater that face each other west of the Chiang Kai-shek Memorial in Taibei. In a scene reminiscent of the Tiananmen Square freedom demonstrations that had met with such brutal repression on mainland China just eight months before, the students sported headbands and shouted slogans in communicating their demands for greater democracy. Concretely, they called for an end to the National Assembly, the retirement of key mainland power figures, an overhaul of the constitution, and a timetable for the transition to a fully democratic state. That same month Lee Teng-hui was elected president of the Republic of China by the same National Assembly that the demonstrators were trying to terminate; after the election, the first for Lee since automatically replacing Chiang in 1988, he felt that he stood on the solid ground necessary to activate his sympathy for the essence, and many of the specifics, of the students' demands.[62]

From June 28 to July 4, 1990, Lee presided over a National Affairs Conference that did much to send Taiwan further down the road toward democracy. Conference attendees expressed genuine agreement that the National Assembly in its current form had outlived its usefulness and that the whole structure of central governance on Taiwan had to be simplified, rationalized, and democratized so as to truly represent the island's citizens and meet their contemporary needs. Attendees also strongly agreed that local governments had to be transformed into more representative, less artificially factionalized institutions. There was consensus, as well, on the need to make substantial changes in the constitution; some even argued that an entirely new constitution be written so as to recognize a new social contract between the government and the people. And though the precise nature of Taiwan's relationship with the mainland would always be the touchiest of all subjects, conference attendees fundamentally agreed that the two sides needed to engage in dialogue, that the format should be one that recognized the government of Taiwan as a partner of equal standing in the discussions, and that peaceful resolution of the conflict in a way that afforded dignity on all sides was in everyone's best interests.[63]

In April 1991 members of the National Assembly voted for measures that made fundamental changes in their own lawmaking body and also in the Legislative Yuan. The Assembly voted to end the outdated "Temporary Provisions Effective during the Period of Mobilization for Suppression of the Communist Rebellion," the lingering existence of which had been inconsistent with the lifting of martial law. The vote to end the provisions symbolized the prevailing will of the Taiwanese leadership to eliminate anachronistic laws and to restructure the government in a way consistent with the realities of the Taiwanese polity in the 1990s. In further fulfill-ment of that will, the National Assembly voted to cut its own membership from 613 to 327 and that of the Legislative Yuan from 220 to 161. And in a move to give the electorate more frequent opportunity to review the per-formance of those making important constitutional policy, the term for members of the National Assembly was reduced from six to four years.[64]

Acrimony continued to arise, though, on the contentious issue of Tai-wanese independence. When the government moved to crack down on those on Taiwan active in the U.S.-based World United Formosans for Independence, the Democratic Progressive Party boldly identified itself as the "party of independence." Although technically that was still a legally proscribed declaration, the Guomindang administration made no move to shut the opposition party down or to prevent any of its candidates from running in the December 1991 elections for a now very different Taiwanized National Assembly. This probably reflected Lee Teng-hui's genuine democratic spirit, but as it turned out it could have been a cool reflection that the Democratic Progressive Party was moving too fast in its advocacy of independence. Later, that stance would appear less threat-ening to an increasingly emboldened electorate, but in late 1991 it did not play well. In the elections for the new National Assembly, the Guomin-dang gained 254 seats and the Democratic Progressive Party won 66 seats, while the remaining 7 seats went to candidates not affiliated with either party.[65]

Rather than gloating in victory, though, a now more progressive mem-bership acted so as to project the Guomindang as the proponent of sensi-ble reform. Events moved very fast in 1992. During the winter, the Guomindang signaled that a very new day was at hand by issuing a report on the February 28th Incident. To the Taiwanese people, the report came 45 years late, but the report was factual and the final statement embedded in the report was contrite. Discussions began on the building of a memorial to stand in a public place as a reminder of the incident, its injustice, and the suffering endured by the Taiwanese people.[66]

As the Guomindang moved to capture the support of that part of the Tai-wanese populace that was inclined to form the more moderate portion of the Democratic Progressive Party's constituency, the opposition party issued its own positions and kept its own presence firmly in the public eye. A Democratic Progressive Party white paper argued for a "One China-One

Taiwan" position that would give the island political independence rather than incorporation into the political system prevailing on the mainland. The opposition party also called for direct transportation links to the mainland, to replace the encumbering necessity of going through Hong Kong that had prevailed since the ruling party had lifted the ban on travel to mainland China. The Democratic Progressive Party also called for a host of reforms to overhaul the political system on Taiwan. The party argued for the design and implementation of a thoroughgoing social security system. It called for substantial changes in the education curricula at all levels, in which objective information was to supplant the propaganda that suffused materials in the social sciences and literature. The party's white paper also presented the outlines of plans to advance the cause and rights of labor and to bring greater attention to the needs of the underclass. And in this position paper the Democratic Progressive Party demanded that the Guomindang and its government disinvest in the enterprises that monopolized key industries, brought in so much revenue, and entrenched the power of the ruling party.[67]

In late May, the National Assembly passed several measures that furthered the cause of reform. The Assembly voted to shorten terms in both its own legislature and in the Legislative Yuan. The Control Yuan, previously one of the five main components of the central governing branches, was assigned to a lower rung than that occupied by the Legislative, Executive, Judicial, and Examination Yuan. In another reform move, the National Assembly deemed that the provincial governor and county magistrates would now be elected directly by citizens; previously, provincial governor was an office appointed by the president with the approval of the National Assembly, while the county magistrate positions were filled by those elected at the behest of township representatives. The National Assembly also appointed a 15-member court to review political party activities.[68]

As the ruling party anticipated the electoral challenge for Legislative Yuan seats in fall 1992, it affirmed its commitment to a One China policy and eventual reunion with the mainland. At the same time, though, Lee Teng-hui and other Guomindang officials stressed the internationalization theme in the articulation of foreign policy, clearly indicating that the government meant to use Taiwan's status as an important player in international trade to help it break through the diplomatic barriers that had limited its room to maneuver in international politics since the 1970s. Leaders also touted the reform efforts that the party was making and emphasized how the very election for national legislative positions demonstrated the Guomindang's commitment to a newly democratized and liberalized Taiwan. As compelling as these themes were, they did not prevent the Democratic Progressive Party from making significant gains in the fall 1992 elections. The opposition party garnered 47 percent of the popular vote and won 50 seats in the Legislative Yuan. Voting patterns across districts, and the way that voting districts were drawn, allowed the Guomindang to secure 102 seats. But the Guomindang's receipt of only 53 percent of the popular vote sent the ruling party the strongest message yet as to the growing strength of its political rival.[69]

By the middle 1990s, it had become clear that the government's attention to matters of infrastructure, research, development, and smooth transitions to higher and higher levels of technological sophistication had yielded great results for the island's economy. With science and industrial parks on the model of the nonpareil Xinzhu complex, and with the transportation, communication, power generation, and port facilities necessary to a thriving economy, Taiwanese businesspeople were able to make the necessary adjustments in production structure and production techniques that would keep Taiwan competitive on the international marketplace. Ironically, the government's very success on the economic front allowed the pent-up emotions of the Taiwanese people to manifest themselves ever more insistently in public places. Farmers, young people, women, intellectuals, artists, and aborigines all clamored for changes that would better incorporate their interests and concerns into the life of the maturing society.[70]

Farmers were restive over the status of agriculture, which continued to slip in relation to industry and commerce. Despite efforts to move into higher-value crops and to shift a great deal of production into fish-farming, vegetables, flowers, eels, and other products with the potential for high yields and profits on farms of small surface area, a career in agriculture held little appeal for young people, and farmers continued to lament their position relative to other participants in the island's economic life. And while environmentalists sometimes clashed with these same farmers on hog-farming practices and applications of chemicals to the soil, they made common cause on the matter of encroachment on scarce land by builders of golf courses, apartment buildings, planned communities sprawling into the suburbs and beyond, and industries still given to polluting air and water. Students across the island continued to demand higher levels of democratization and a greater voice on matters pertinent to college and university life. Feminists pressed their cause more fervently than ever, and their efforts were resulting in major attitudinal shifts in the workplace, where women were gaining representation in fields that had always been exclusive male provinces.[71]

Artists and intellectuals made a major impact on the temper of the times in 1990s Taiwan. With the economy bustling and the ruling party scrambling to find its way in a more liberalized political system, artists and intellectuals felt a great deal of freedom to press for advances in the island's long-neglected cultural sphere. Such pressures had begun to find application in the 1980s, when the construction of the National Theater and the National Concert Hall symbolized the greater attention that was being given to cultural matters. The construction of the Museum of Fine Arts in Taibei, with great space given to contemporary works that addressed the anxieties and preoccupations of people caught up in a whirlwind of change, also was symbolically and substantively important in the drive for higher cultural standards on the island. Similarly, a fine new Museum of Science in Taizhong provided room for displays that could enthrall the most sophisticated visitors from the most culturally advanced nations in the world. Poets, novelists, and calligraphers experimented with new forms and embraced the search for identity that was everywhere evident among the people of Taiwan. Craftspersons both sought to preserve the legacy of the island's cultural inheritance and made dramatic new contributions to the arts of glass-making, pottery, ceramics, and textiles. New museums that sprang up in Taibei and Gaoxiong did considerable justice to preserving the culture of the indigenous people, and a major new development in the area of Sun Moon Lake at the island's center authentically preserved the dwelling styles and physical culture of the aborigines in a very dignified setting.[72]

During the 1990s these indigenous people came together as never before to assert their rights and to fight for their interests in the democratized polity of Taiwan. The process had actually begun in 1985 with the founding of the Alliance of Taiwanese Aborigines under the leadership of Yi-chiang Pa-lu-erh, a member of the Ami aboriginal group. At first the organization focused on grievances such as encroachment by business and government institutions on aborigine lands and the recruitment of young aboriginal women by Han Chinese prostitution rings. But a visit by the leaders of the Presbyterian Church of Taiwan to the Philippines in May 1987 dramatically changed the course of the aborigine rights movement. In their visit with the Cordillera People's Alliance, the Taiwanese group came into contact with a copy of the "Statement of Principles of the World Council of Indigenous Peoples" that this international organization had drafted a few months before. When Yi-chiang Pa-lu-erh received a copy of the statement sent by the Presbyterian group, one line in particular resonated with him: the proclamation that "all indigenous people have the right to self-determination and can freely determine the direction of their own development." This prompted Yi-chiang Pa-lu-erh to write an editorial in the June 1987 issue of *Yuanzhumin* (*Aborigines,* the chief journal addressing the concerns of all of Taiwan's indigenous people), proclaiming for the first time what would come to be an article of faith among the aborigines: The aborigines of Taiwan had the right to self-government, determining the course of their own affairs in all matters except foreign policy and defense.[73]

Over the succeeding years what had first been a bold and radical assertion even among aborigine moderates came to be a commonly accepted idea among Taiwan's indigenous people. The group worked out the precise boundaries of an area in the mountainous spine and along the eastern coast of Taiwan that was to comprise the self-governing unit. Yi-chiang Pa-luerh attended the United Nations Working Group on Indigenous Populations in Geneva in July 1991; he came away with a bolstered faith in the justice of the self-government movement, and he asserted that the relevant term describing the aborigines broadly construed should be *yuanzhu minzu* ("indigenous peoples"), a refinement of the term *yuanzhumin* ("indigenous people") that for years the aborigines had been pushing to replace the term *shanbao* ("mountain compatriots") used by the majority of Han Chinese. The latest refinement has not yet gained wide usage in Taiwanese society, but the *yuanzhumin* name has replaced the older *shanbaomin* term.[74]

The push for self-government has grown incessant. In December 1993 a heavyweight group of aboriginal professors, church officials, heads of civic organizations, township mayors, and legislators from the Legislative Yuan, National Assembly, and Provincial Assembly came together in a Taiwan Aboriginal Policy and Social Development Consultative Conference to press their concerns with Han Chinese attendees in a position to affect policy in the area of aboriginal affairs. An array of ideas relevant to advancing the self-government theme were put forward and gained a sympathetic hearing from the Han Chinese in attendance. The wheels of action on these ideas turned very slowly, but one idea that did come to fruition three years later was the notion of an Aborigine Affairs Commission to be established within the Executive Yuan. A bill bringing this into the governmental framework of the Republic of China was passed in the Legislative Yuan in July 1996, and in time local aborigine affairs commissions were established in Taibei and Gaoxiong. In August 1996 a group of notables came together as the Taiwan Aborigine Self-Government Working Group for a visit to Canada to examine the achievements of the Canadian First Nations. The group returned to Taiwan emboldened by the notion that self-government is a self-evident fact founded upon aborigine self-identity; practical considerations aside, it is not something that any other government gives or takes away. This most aggressive statement of the self-government concept has now gained wide acceptance among the indigenous peoples themselves. Although the government of the Republic of China has not yet moved as far in the direction of granting self-government as the aborigines would like, both the Guomindang and the Democratic Progressive Party court the aborigine vote and show increasing sensitivity to aborigine concerns. On an island where there exists an energetic quest for national identity, the effort to describe what it means to be Taiwanese now takes into consideration the culture of the aboriginal peoples, who have a place alongside those whose ancestors came to Taiwan centuries ago and those whose families arrived only after 1945.[75]

Startling political developments brought an increasingly fast-paced march toward a politically competitive democracy on Taiwan as a new millennium loomed. In 1994 the Legislative Yuan passed a law bringing directly elected mayoral positions to the cities of Taibei and Gaoxiong for the first time. In December of that year, Democratic Progressive Party activist Chen Shuibian won the race for mayor of Taibei. This victory was a harbinger of even greater change to come. By the mid-1990s another political party, the New Party, composed of young, reformist, but steadfast One China renegades of the Guomindang, emerged as a significant political player. In December 1995 elections for the Legislative Yuan, the Guomindang mustered only 46.06 percent of the vote, while the Democratic Progressive Party came on strong at 33.17 percent and the New Party registered 12.95 percent. This set the stage for the first very competitive popular election for president of the Republic of China in March 1996. Lee Teng-hui gained a convincing victory, winning 54 percent of the votes in that election. But renegade Guomindang candidates Lin Yanggang and Zhen Lian registered 14.9 percent and 10 percent respectively. And Democratic Progressive Party candidate Peng Mingmin, with his 21 percent, demonstrated that at least that many Taiwanese were ready to entertain the notion of the island as a nation officially independent of the mainland. That notion gained greater and greater credence as the island's people prepared to greet the year 2000.[76]

In spring 2000 the Taiwanese people weighed carefully the campaign stances of the candidates for the republic's presidency, only the second in which the popular vote would determine the outcome. President Lee Teng-hui had announced his retirement from the office, throwing his support to the Guomindang candidate, Lien Chan. As the Guomindang standard-bearer associated with policy statements of Lee, Lien's position on relations with the mainland had him embracing the traditional One China notion of eventual reunification but greatly amending this stance with language consistent with the "two states" theory pronounced by Lee Teng-hui and denounced by the communist government of mainland China. In July 1999 Lee advanced the notion that according to current reality in cross-straits relations, the governments of Taiwan and mainland China had come to act on the international stage as discrete political entities; any discussions about future reunification had to ensue as a dialogue between equals. This had angered the mainland government, which interpreted Lee's statement as courting pro-independence sentiment. While Lien Chan was necessarily associated with Lee's statements as the Guomindang candidate in the presidential campaign, the other candidates carved out their own positions.[77]

Independent candidate James Soong, having just been booted from the Guomindang for running against the party-backed candidate, took a position closer to the more hard-line approach of the Guomindang of yester-year. He stood firmly behind eventual reunification, though even he spoke in language emphasizing Taiwan's refusal to be bullied by the mainland regime. Another independent candidate, Xu Xinliang, a breakaway not from the ruling party but rather from the Democratic Progressive Party, offered a different and surprising stance as the election neared. A veteran independence activist, Xu nevertheless assessed the growing tension between the mainland and Taiwan and suggested that Taiwanese negotiators sign an agreement with their mainland counterparts that would guarantee the status quo under the One China principle for 50 years. Rounding out the roster of candidates was Chen Shuibian, the Democratic Progressive Party candidate who carried his party's pro-independence heritage into the campaign. Chen offered a position that in no way denied that heritage or the rectitude of the stance but left him with potentially more room to maneuver than any other candidate: To a skeptical mainland government but a very attentive Taiwanese populace, Chen said that he would not declare Taiwan's independence unless the mainland regime militarily attacked the island.[78]

Chen Shuibian also made a convincing case that he would clean up the island's atmosphere, in both environmental and political aspects. Most important to his election chances was his pledge to investigate Guomindang-controlled business enterprises, insider trading, and investment tips and opportunities long dispensed by the incumbent regime for the benefit of highly placed Guomindang and government officials. This message gained a very receptive hearing among influential members of Taiwan's business community such as Xu Wenlong of petrochemical giant Chi Mei, Stan Shih of the Acer Group, and Zong Yongfa of the Evergreen Group. Chen also endeared himself to environmentalists and villagers of rural Taibei county, where a fourth nuclear power plant was due for completion: He pledged to nix the $6 billion project and explore alternative energy sources instead.[79]

Chen's diplomatic flexibility, firm dedication to the political dignity of Taiwan, plans for business reform, and environmentalist stance proved to be a winning combination. As the election grew near, polls showed that the voting public was ready for a change in political leadership. This boded ill for Lien Chan, so closely tied as he was to the Guomindang establishment. A taint of investment scandal in the family of James Soong undermined his squeaky-clean image and his front-runner status. Xu Xinliang had no chance; polls showed him likely to garner no more than 2 percent of the vote. All of this worked to the advantage of Chen, who stunned domestic and international observers with a narrow victory when tallies from the March 18, 2000, presidential contest were totaled.[80]

In the aftermath of his advocacy of the "two states" theory, Lee Teng-hui had elicited abundant criticism from the government of the People's Republic of China, but his party was still a known quantity that continued to formally adhere to the notion of One China. Chen Shuibian, on the other hand, led a party with an identity intrinsically tied to its call for an independent Taiwan. Though Chen adopted a moderate version of his party's typical stance, his election was the result that the mainland regime had wanted least; indeed, the government of the People's Republic had issued numerous statements to warn the Taiwanese people not to vote Chen in as president, going so far as to threaten war should Chen take office and declare Taiwan's independence. But at his inaugural ceremony on May 20, 2000, Chen gave a brilliant speech that reiterated his vow not to declare Taiwan's independence unless the mainland government chose rash military action to bend the island polity to its will. Further, Chen invited the mainland leadership to visit Taiwan, called for a resumption of talks to work toward a resolution of tensions, and in many ways took a far more conciliatory stance than observers in many quarters might have expected. Within Taiwan, Chen Shuibian maintained high approval ratings right through the summer as the economy grew nearly 7 percent, the inflation rate remarkably came in under 1 percent, and unemployment stayed under 3 percent. Chen also gave evidence of sticking to his campaign promises. His government launched investigations into the acquisition of "black gold," money obtained through such shady practices as insider trading and undercollateralized bank loans to those favored by the Guomindang. Though moving more cautiously than many in his environmentalist constituency wanted, he showed follow-through on his environmental cleanup pledge too: He set up a committee to study the nuclear power plant question and by fall 2000 seemed headed toward a decision to nix the project.[81]

By that autumn of 2000, the honeymoon of Chen Shuibian as president of the island republic was clearly over. Battles with a still Guomindang-dominated legislature loomed. Chen experienced difficulties both with his vice president, Annette Lu (Lu Xiulian), who tended to make public statements at odds with Chen's moderate pronouncements, and with Tang Fei, the Guomindang member and former defense minister whom Chen had tapped as premier, in what had seemed a brilliant political stroke. Chen did move to moderate the vice president's statements and curb her independent streak, but he could not save the Tang cabinet from internal bickering and gridlock. The stock market declined precipitously in October 2000, though all other economic indicators remained strong. Chen promptly elevated Deputy Premier Zhang Zhunxiong, a Democratic Progressive Party veteran and highly respected adviser, to the premiership. He also added several people with abundant experience in economic and financial management to his cabinet. Most Taiwanese continued to view the president favorably, willing to give him the time needed to guide the government of Taiwan through its first drastic change in leadership in 55 years.[82]

With the election of Chen Shuibian as president and a generally successful first few months under Democratic Progressive Party leadership, Taiwan was no longer under Guomindang rule. As the island's people looked to the twenty-first century, they could be proud of their bold vote in March 2000. A leadership bred on the island and a political party launched in the context of the contemporary struggle for democracy at last held power on Taiwan. After centuries under the outsider regimes of the Dutch, the Zheng family, the Qing, the Japanese, and the Guomindang, the Taiwanese people now ruled their own island. They knew that their island polity was an independent nation in all but name. And they knew that however prudent they and their leadership continued to be for the foreseeable future, there abided in the history of the land they called home a convincing case for independence.

NOTES

1. Zhou Mingfeng, *Taiwan jian* shi [A concise history of Taiwan] (Taibei: Qian Wei Press, 1994), p. 96 and pp. 105–8; Wang Xiaobo, *Taiwan shi yu Taiwan ren* [Taiwanese history and the Taiwanese people] (Taibei: Dongda Books, 1988), pp. 113–30, 131–35, 157–68, and 169–99.

2. Zhou Mingfeng, pp. 94–96; 104–8.; Steven Philips, "Between Assimilation and Independence: Taiwanese Political Aspirations under Nationalist Chinese Rule, 1945–1948," in Murray Rubinstein, ed., *Taiwan: A New History* (Armonk, N.Y.: M.E. Sharpe, 1999), p. 282.

3. Zhou Mingfeng, pp. 102–9; Philips, p. 282.

4. Zhou Mingfeng, pp. 109–18; Philips, p. 291.

5. Zhou Mingfeng, pp. 112–25; Philips, pp. 288–89.

6. Zhou Mingfeng, pp. 115–18; Philips, p. 290.

7. Zhou Mingfeng, pp. 118–21, Philips, pp. 291–92.

8. Zhou Mingfeng, pp. 121–22.

9. Zhou Mingfeng, pp. 122–25; Philips, pp. 293–94.

10. Zhou Mingfeng, pp. 125–27; Philips, p. 295.

11. Zhou Mingfeng, pp. 123–29; Philips, p. 295.

12. Zhou Mingfeng, pp. 124–33; Philips, p. 296.

13. Zhou Mingfeng, pp. 133–37; Phillips, p. 297.

14. Zhou Mingfeng, pp. 137–38; Philips, p. 298.

15. Zhou Mingfeng, pp. 139–48; Philips, p. 300.

16. Lin Zhongxiong, *Taiwan jingji fazhan sishinian* [Forty years in the economic development of Taiwan] (Taibei: Zili Evening News, 1987), p. 29.

17. Peter Chen-main Wang, "A Bastion Created, a Regime Reformed, an Economy Reengineered, 1949–1970," in Rubinstein, p. 321.

18. Ibid., pp. 321–22.

19. Han Lih-wu, *Taiwan Today* (Taibei: Cheng Chung Book Co., 1988), pp. 20–22.

20. Ibid., pp. 22–24.

21. Ibid., pp. 20–22.

22. Peter Chen-main Wang, p. 323.

23. Gary Marvin Davison, *Agricultural Development and the Fate of Farmers in Taiwan, 1945–1990* (Minneapolis: Ph.D. diss., University of Minnesota, 1993), pp. 77–106, discusses the Guomindang strategy for economic development that took shape during the 1950s.

24. Lin Zhongxiong, pp. 29–35.

25. Yin Zhangfu, *Zhongguo zhi tudi gaige* [The land reform of China], (Taibei: Central Research Materials Agency, 1984), pp. 107–9.

26. Qi Jialin, pp. 181–234; Wu Congxian, *Zhongguo nongye fazhan* [Chinese agricultural development] (Taibei: Central Research Documents Center), pp. 511–13; Lin Zhongxiong, pp. 41–45; Huang Junjie, *Taiwan nongcun de huanghun*

[The twlight of Taiwanese agriculture] (Taibei: Zili Evening News, 1988), pp. 50–51; Yin Zhangfu, pp. 64–76.

27. Wu Congxian, p. 513; Xiao Guoho, *Taiwan nongye xingshuai sishi nian* [Forty years in the rise and fall of Taiwanese agriculture] (Taibei: Zili Evening News, 1988), p. 132; Yin Zhangfu, pp. 76–84.

28. Wu Congxian, pp. 513–17; Yin Zhangfu, pp. 90–99.

29. Wu Congxian, pp. 513–17; Yin Zhangfu, pp. 100–104.

30. Wu Congxian, pp. 367–70; Lin Zhongxiong, pp. 51, 56, 74, and 79–100.

31. Li Songlin, in his *Jiang Jingguo de shidai* [The Chiang Ching-kuo era] (Taibei: Fenglin Shidai, Ltd., 1993), pp. 1–2, discusses the temper of the times and Chiang Ching-kuo's role on Taiwan during the 1950s and early 1960s.

32. Peter Chen-main Wang, pp. 327–28.

33. Lin Zhongxiong, pp. 38–45; Peter Chen-main Wang, pp. 328–29.

34. Davison, pp. 78–89; Peter Chen-main Wang, p. 329.

35. Davison, p. 81; Lin Zhongxiong, p. 49; Peter Chen-main Wang, p. 329.

36. Davison, pp. 90–91; Lin Zhongxiong, pp. 58–61; Peter Chen-main Wang, pp. 331–32.

37. Davison, p. 92; Lin Zhongxiong, pp. 59–61; Peter Chen-main Wang, p. 332.

38. Davison, pp. 91–92.

39. Huang Dashou, pp. 339–343.

40. Davison, p. 91; Lin Zhongxiong, pp. 59–61; Peter Chen-main Wang, pp. 332–33.

41. Davison, pp. 92–96; Lin Zhongxiong, pp. 61–77; Peter Chen-main Wang, pp. 332–33.

42. Davison, pp. 117-18; Lin Zhongxiong, pp. 79–81.

43. Ibid.

44. Davison, pp. 118–19; Lin Zhongxiong, pp. 79–83.

45. Gary Marvin Davison and Barbara E. Reed, *Culture and Customs of Taiwan* (Westport, Conn.: Greenwood Press, 1998), p. 23; Lin Zhongxiong, pp. 84–89.

46. Davison, pp. 122–23. Li Songlin, pp. 23–31, gives a detailed discussion of the 10 major projects.

47. Peter Chen-main Wang, p. 335.

48. Rubinstein, p. 437. See Li Songlin, pp. 31–37, for commentary on Chiang Ching-kuo's adroit Taiwanization of the Guomindang and his policies designed to meet the demands of broad sectors of Taiwanese society during the 1980s. See also Li Songlin's commentary, pp. 37–43, on Chiang Ching-kuo's assumption of the presidency in 1975.

49. Sung-sheng Yvonne Chang, "Literature in Post-1949 Taiwan, 1950–1980s," in Rubinstein, pp. 412–16.

50. See pp. 439–43 of Murray A. Rubinstein's "Taiwan's Socioeconomic Modernization," one of his own articles in *Taiwan: A New History;* and on the Zhongli Incident, see Li Songlin, pp. 48–52.

51. Rubinstein, pp. 441–43. Li Songlin, pp. 52–58, covers the Gaoxiong *Meili dao* Incident in some detail.

52. Li Songlin, pp. 151–78, examines the various pressures and influences that induced Chiang Ching-kuo to move more aggressively toward political transformation on Taiwan with the approach of the middle 1980s.

53. During my dissertation research period of 1988–90 on Taiwan, two of the island's foremost scholars of the Taiwanese farmers' movement and the contemporary Taiwanese farmers' dilemma, Hsiao Hsin-huang and Huang Chun-chieh, were kind enough to give me articles they had written, which greatly increased my understanding of the Taiwanese farmers' movement and in general helped me understand the context for the various social movements on Taiwan during the 1980s. The article penned by Professor Hsiao, handed to me during a personal interview August 10, 1990, is *"Taiwan de nongmin yundong: jian tan yan yangchu pingjiao sixiang de xiandai qishi"* [The farmers' movement on Taiwan: Simultaneously discussing the contemporary revelations of the thought of Yan Yangzhou on mass education], which Professor Hsiao delivered as a talk at the International Symposium on the Thought of Dr. Yan Yangzhou Regarding Mass Education and Rural Reform. Professor Huang's article, handed to me during a personal interview August 7, 1990, is *"Zhan hou taiwan nongmin nongye ishi de jianbian"* [The shift of the agricultural consciousness of farmers in postwar Taiwan], reprinted from *Jindai zhongguo nongcun jingji shi lunji* [Collection of essays on modern Chinese rural economic history] (Taibei: Modern Chinese History Research Institute, Academia Sinica, 1989), pp. 21–43.

54. Rubinstein, p. 446.

55. Ibid., pp. 446–47. Li Songlin, pp. 179–213, gives an excellent detailed description and analysis of Chiang Ching-kuo's lifting of martial law; see pp. 204–13 for his legalization of opposition parties.

56. Rubinstein, p. 447.

57. Ibid., pp. 373–74; Davison, pp. 122 and 126–27.

58. Davison, pp. 138–39; Rubinstein, pp. 375–76.

59. Rubinstein, pp. 447–48.

60. Ibid., pp. 448–49.

61. Ibid., pp. 449–50. See Li Songlin, pp. 265–69 for an examination of Lee Teng-hui's agenda in the years just after he assumed the presidency.

62. Rubinstein, pp. 450–51.

63. Ibid., pp. 451–52.

64. Ibid., p. 454. Li Songlin, pp. 282–87, examines Lee Teng-hui's response to the Taiwan independence movement of the late 1980s and early 1990s.

65. Rubinstein, pp. 454–55.

66. Ibid., p. 456.

67. Ibid., p. 456. The Democratic Progressive Party would shift to a status quo position on the direct travel ban as the 1990s progressed. As the People's Republic of China government failed to recognize Taiwan as a diplomatic equal, the

Democratic Progressive Party leadership sought to slow the pace of cross-strait interaction. See Leng Tse-Kang, *The Taiwan-China Connection: Democracy and Development Across the Taiwan Straits* (Boulder, CO: Westview Press, 1996), pp. 42–45.

68. Ibid., pp. 455–56.

69. Ibid., p. 457.

70. Ibid., pp. 376–77.

71. Davison, pp. 154–72.

72. Observations during personal visits, summer 1995 and summer 1998; Davison and Reed, pp. 91–118.

73. Michael Stainton, "Aboriginal Self-Government: Taiwan's Uncompleted Agenda," in Rubinstein, pp. 422–23.

74. Ibid., pp. 424–25.

75. Ibid., pp. 425–29.

76. Susan V. Lawrence and Julian Baum, "Jaw Jaw, Else War War," *Far Eastern Economic Review,* 2 March 2000, pp. 20–22.

77. Julian Baum, "Psst! We're All Chinese," *Far Eastern Economic Review,* 2 March 2000, p. 23.

78. Ibid. For details on the scandal that engulfed Soong, see Julian Baum's article, "Soong Sullied: Money Politics Scandal Hits Presidential Front-Runner," *Far Eastern Economic Review,* 30 December 1999–6 January 2000.

79. Julian Baum, Dan Biers, and Susan V. Lawrence, "Chen's Chance," *Far Eastern Economic Review,* 30 March 2000, pp. 18–20.

80. Julian Baum and Bruce Gilley, "Crude Tactics," *Far Eastern Economic Review,* 29 June 2000, p. 25.

81. Julian Baum and Dan Biers, "The New-Look KMT, Inc.," *Far Eastern Economic Review,* 9 March 2000, pp. 42–46; and Julian Baum, "Nuclear Test," *Far Eastern Economic Review,* 8 June 2000, p. 20.

82. Phil Revzin, Michael Vatikiotis, David Plott, and Ben Dolven, "Lee: The Cruel Game," *Far Eastern Economic Review,* 8 June 2000, pp. 17–18; "Chen Stands by VP," from the "Intelligence" section of *Far Eastern Economic Review,* 29 June 2000, p. 8.

Chapter 7

TAIWANESE RULE IN THE YEAR 2000 AND BEYOND: THE CASE FOR INDEPENDENCE

Taiwan will be an independent nation if the island's people decide that it should be. Within the realities of regional political and military circumstance, this is true for any people who feel an intense national bond formed from some combination of shared linguistic, religious, historical, or broad cultural traits. In the face of countervailing political and military forces objecting to a declaration of independence, a people's justification for making the claim to nationhood is stronger or weaker depending on the cultural uniqueness and territorial identification that have prevailed through a significant stretch of history.

The historical differences between Taiwan and mainland China are compelling. Humans living in the Yellow River valley of northern China began to assemble the essential elements of Chinese civilization in the course of the second millennium B.C. By the end of the first millennium B.C., the people of the great Han dynasty (202 B.C.–A.D. 220) brought those elements of Chinese civilization together in a distinct style that would endure in its most essential features into the first decade of the twentieth century A.D. This distinct and enduring civilization was imperial China. Imperial China of course witnessed tremendous cultural change and technological advance as history brought forth the distinctive Sui, Tang, Song, Yuan, Ming, and Qing dynasties; but certain core cultural features remained continuous over at least two thousand years of civilization on mainland China. And it is possible to make the case that the essential features of those who came to be known as the Han people had been in place long before the Han dynasty itself brought those features together in such an enduring governing style.

For most of these centuries, Taiwan was occupied almost exclusively by people who spoke Malayo-Polynesian dialects and bore more cultural similarity to the peoples of Southeast Asian and Pacific islands than they did to the inhabitants of mainland China. Han people traversed the Taiwan strait in significant numbers only very late in the imperial history of China. The first ruling authorities to impose their governing will upon the Han Chinese and the aboriginal inhabitants of Taiwan were not from mainland China. The Dutch and the Zheng family regimes wielded governing authority on Taiwan before the Manchus, ironically a non-Han people who formed a long-lived (1644–1912) Chinese-style dynasty, first included Taiwan among the territorial claims of imperial China in 1684. But for the verbal exertions of the official Shi Lang, the Qing court might have decided to abandon Taiwan and exclude it from the territorial map of imperial China. When in 1895 Japanese negotiators at Shimonoseki demanded Taiwan as a spoil of war, the Qing court relinquished the island without much protest. Between these bookend years of 1684 and 1895, Qing officials strove mightily to direct the energies of fractious Hakka, Quanzhou, Zhangzhou, and aborigine subethnic groups toward productive economic endeavors and away from violent attacks on each other or the representatives of officialdom. But uprisings against Qing officials occurred frequently and, in the cases of the Zhu Yigui (1721) and Lin Shuangwen (1787–1788) rebellions posed truly serious challenges to imperial authority on Taiwan.

For a variety of reasons, the Qing administrative apparatus on Taiwan grew tighter in the course of the nineteenth century. Qing authorities had duly received the message that discontent among the Taiwanese people persisted and could bubble up from below the surface to manifest itself overtly, in ways that threatened dynastic authority and political stability on the island. Would-be rebels, for their part, could not help but be impressed by the ultimate message delivered by the Qing forces at the end of the Zhu and Lin episodes: When faced with large-scale challenge, the military might of the governing authority from the mainland was likely to prevail. Localized disturbances continued to occur throughout the nineteenth century, but there were no rebellions of anything near the scope of those waged by Zhu and Lin. If internal developments had not been enough to increase the Qing officials' alertness and attention to administrative detail, international political, military, and commercial pressures worked even more persistently to upgrade the dynasty's concern for the fate of Taiwan.

In the aftermath of the Opium Wars, British, French, and Japanese forces especially brought such pressures to bear on the people of both mainland China and the island of Taiwan.

Dynastic concern for the increasingly strategic outposts of Taiwan led the Qing regime to send Liu Mingchuan to Taiwan and to upgrade the island's long-held status as a mere prefecture of Fujian province to that of a province in its own right. Furthermore, Taiwan's favorable location and historical orientation to the outside world in matters of international trade led the officials of the Qing to make the island a showcase for the dynasty's program of self-strengthening, by which it hoped to counter the military and technological power of the Western nations that evidenced a disturbing tendency to meddle in both mainland Chinese and Taiwanese affairs. Late in the Qing dynasty's rule, especially during the 1884–91 period of Liu Mingchuan's governorship, Taiwan did become the most technologically and commercially modernized area under Qing authority. In the end, though, the self-strengthening effort was not enough. The years after Liu Mingchuan's administration of the island saw a general retrenchment in efforts to build a modern infrastructure on Taiwan. This insufficient response to the challenges of modernity soon resulted in a disastrous military setback. The Chinese loss to the Japanese in the war of 1894–1895, spurred by events in Korea and competition for influence there, was momentous for many reasons. The loss set in motion a series of events that led to the fall of the Qing and the Chinese imperial system and that reinforced and advanced the development of Taiwan as a unique entity apart from mainland China.

Taiwan came under Japanese governance from 1895 to 1945, years that roughly encompassed the first half of the twentieth century. This was no ordinary period in human history. With each passing year of the extraordinary century, change came to the world with unprecedented rapidity; thus, on an island controlled by Japan, the people of Taiwan came face-to-face with modern change as delivered in the Japanese style. Cut off from the mainland, the people of Taiwan searched in literary, artistic, and other cultural realms for an authentic identity that necessarily had to be defined in a colonial context controlled by the Japanese. Significantly, those at the forefront of the search for identity gave little evidence of a longing for reunion with mainland China. Most typically, they sought self-rule and cultural integrity for Taiwan within the broader context of Japanese imperial rule. By the late 1930s and early 1940s, many Taiwanese had resigned themselves to Japanese control. The most common demand by those making the case for Taiwanese self-rule was for a position of distinction and autonomy in matters of internal affairs on the island, with recognition that the realms of military and foreign affairs lay incontestably under the authority of the Japanese.

Taiwanese reaction, then, to the Japanese defeat in World War II was mixed. For the many Taiwanese who had served in the Japanese military or who had otherwise loyally supported the colonial regime, the defeat was their own. Others, weary from the economic travails of the wartime years, embraced change and took heart at the Japanese exit. Some, learning that the mainland Chinese power as represented by the Guomindang had come to govern Taiwan, felt that fellow ethnic Han Chinese would bring a gentler style of rule and an amelioration of the harsh conditions that had prevailed under the rain of American bombs. Then, as the Guomindang manifested all the traits that were causing it to forfeit control of mainland China to the communists, many in the Taiwanese leadership, including those who had led the self-rule movement during the colonial years, turned against the Guomindang government. They made the same essential pitch for self-rule to the Guomindang authorities that they had made to the Japanese and, for good measure, let the Guomindang authorities know that the most common view among the Taiwanese people was that life had actually been better under the Japanese than it was in the late 1940s under the Guomindang.

The Guomindang formulated its response under the pressures of the unfortunate February 28th Incident. The hammer came down, knocking out virtually all potential dissidents. Those Taiwanese people who survived the incident relatively unscathed cowered in their homes, angry but subdued. During the 1950s and 1960s the Guomindang gave many Taiwanese people reason to see the regime in a more favorable light, so that a common view among outside observers as the island entered the 1970s and even the 1980s was that the people had been bought off and won to the administrative authority of the Guomindang. But when that very economic success that had seemingly proven so politically effective for the ruling authorities gave middle-class folk the time and leisure to turn their attention to political affairs, the underlying tensions that had never been resolved in the aftermath of the February 28th Incident became manifest, at first in the actions of a courageous few, and then in the open proclamations and occasional demonstrations of the middle-class majority.

By July 1987, martial law was no more. By 1988, the island had its first Taiwanese president in the context of postwar Guomindang rule. By 1990 this man, Lee Teng-hui, who had replaced Chiang Ching-kuo upon the latter's death, was elected by the National Assembly. Lee superintended the democratization of the political system and won the presidency in 1996 under the new and invigorating conditions of a popular vote. In the meantime the right of legitimate contenders to organize and compete in the political arena had been recognized and, in one of the island's most stunning political developments, the Democratic Progressive Party—the most important of the opposition parties—put forward a candidate who claimed victory and the presidency in March 2000.

Chen Shuibian's victory constituted a convincing statement by the Taiwanese people that they were not afraid of the idea of an independent Taiwan, nor would they be intimidated by the mainland communist regime's opposition to an independence candidate. By the time of the extraordinary victory in the spring 2000 election, there was actually a more radically pro-independence party than the Democratic Progressive Party. This party, the Independence Party, called for an immediate declaration of Taiwan's national independence, whereas Chen and his Democratic Progressive Party were willing to wait until the international political climate seemed propitious, willing to let negotiations with representatives of the mainland regime run their course over some indefinite period of time. Chen and his party had moderated their stance since the early 1990s, when Chen had just risen to prominence as the mayor of Taibei. Still, he and the Democratic Progressive Party had not backed away from the fundamental notion of Taiwan as an independent national entity, and the party's moderate appeal for progress toward nationhood with sensitivity to prevailing international realities seemed very consistent with the trend of public opinion on Taiwan. The fact that public opinion had come this far toward favoring an independent Taiwan was nothing short of stunning to observers who had seen Taiwan's people as motivated more by economic than political concerns, content to linger as an odd subset of greater China.

Despite the stock market decline of October 2000, and even though general economic doldrums set in as the international economy took a downturn during 2001, Chen Shuibian and his Democratic Progressive Party continued to enjoy a great deal of support from the Taiwanese citizenry. Chen and his party struggled during the months after the momentous presidential victory of spring 2000 to master the politics of the Legislative Yuan and to fend off attempts by the Guomindang to undermine the new ruling party's credibility. As elections for the Legislative Yuan approached during the fall of 2001, the Guomindang sought to place blame for the sluggish economy on Chen and his party. But Chen Shuibian and his party's slate of candidates effectively countered that the new administration's policies were fundamentally sound and that Taiwan's economic struggles were due to international conditions beyond the control of the administration.

When results from the December 2001 legislative elections came in, they strongly indicated that the political thunder heard in the spring of 2000 would sound ever louder in the years to come. The Democratic Progressive Party increased its representation in the Legislative Yuan from 70 to 87 members, while Guomindang representation fell from 123 to 68. The voters seemed to want better coordination of executive and legislative policy, and through the elections they conveyed the message that they wanted the Democratic Progressive Party to direct that coordination. The election outcome held other interesting results with significant implications for the near future of Taiwanese politics, including the run-up to the presidential election of spring 2004. James Soong's recently formed People First Party (PFP) garnered 46 seats, while Lee Teng-hui's even more recently and hastily assembled Taiwan Solidarity Union took 13 seats. The New Party managed to elect only one candidate and seemed destined for political oblivion at the national level. Although the Democratic Progressive Party did lose a little ground in 23 city and county elections held on the same day, dropping from a hold on 12 such positions to only 9, they held firmly to their southern Taiwan political base, took the northern Taiwan county of Taibei, and also claimed the northeastern county of Ilan. Lee Teng-hui's break with the Guomindang and his initiative to form the Taiwan Solidarity Union, which would closely ally with the Democratic Progressive Party and bolster Chen Shuibian's public standing, was a most dramatic development. With the likelihood of a legislative coalition of the Democratic Progressive Party, the Taiwan Solidarity Union, and at least 13 additional legislators, Chen Shuibian seemed to have the political upper hand as he entered the year 2003 and anticipated his political prospects for the presidential election looming in spring 2004.[1]

Meanwhile, the Taiwanese people pursued their twentieth-century search for identity to the borders of a new millennium. Everywhere the people of Taiwan turned their attention to matters of culture and quality of life that had been neglected in the mad and economically successful rush to modernity. The unique culture that thrived on Taiwan was not anything that could be described by the outmoded term *Republic of China*, whatever the official title still hovering over the island's government. In the minds of many people the title had become the Republic of Taiwan, a society in which full-blown democracy had overwhelmed those who would rule in an autocratic style informed by centuries of the imperial Chinese experience. Chiang Ching-kuo had seen the change coming and removed the strictures of martial law. Lee Teng-hui had with great skill superintended the transition to democracy. Chen Shuibian took full advantage of the liberalized political environment and brought the island closer to a declaration of independence. And, much as they had during the clamor for self-rule in the 1930s phase of the colonial era under Japanese control, practitioners of the literary and visual arts called upon an array of symbols and sources of historical inspiration that referenced above all life on Taiwan, not life on mainland China.

Today, artists utilizing a variety of media explore the problems, the promise, and the purpose of life on the island they love. Calligrapher Lien Te-sen draws upon contemporary Japanese calligraphic styles to render abstract forms of the Chinese character to suggest the chaotic traffic conditions of urban Taiwan as a metaphor for the politically suspended state of the "Unfocusable Republic of China."[2] Short story writer Ah Sheng, in his "The White Jade Ox," tells the tale of an apartment complex doorman of mainlander provenance whose life becomes entwined with an old Taiwanese gentleman whose ancestors are buried beneath the building.[3] Painter Tseng Yu-wen focuses his art on the rural scenes, temple architecture, and images of locally revered deities that he remembers from an earlier, simpler time on Taiwan: "My paintings must have a strong Taiwanese flavor, so when people see them they can feel Taiwan immediately."[4] The poet Chang Shang-hua hosts a radio show that has featured readings of her work accompanied by traditional and modern musical instruments. In "A Sheet of Blotting Paper," a guitar strums movingly as the poem reveals a vulnerability born either of a romantic relationship or the search for cultural identity:

> I am a sheet of blotting paper
> Lightly pressed against the page
> you've written on
> Absorbing the drops you left there.[5]

Practitioners of the folk arts on Taiwan pursue the crafts of paper making, stone carving, woodblock printing, lantern making, and drum making in the unique forms that these have taken on the island.[6] In a major project featuring authentic aboriginal dwellings, cultural exhibits, and performances in music and dance, the Nine Tribes Cultural Village in central Taiwan shows a new attentiveness to the island's original inhabitants that can also be seen in splendid new museums in Taibei and Gaoxiong.[7] The new assertiveness on the part of the aborigines now thrusts their traditions and their arts into the cultural mix from which the Taiwanese people seek to form an identity. An exhibit at the Taibei Fine Arts Museum features the four sources of Taiwanese culture that inform this process of national definition: aboriginal culture, traditional Chinese culture, the cultural legacy of the Japanese colonial period, and the local manifestations of Western culture.[8]

Modernity has come to Taiwan as the island's hardworking people have responded to the conditions and opportunities provided by two governing authorities that arrived from outside the island to impose their regimes on the populace. One of those authorities departed after a half century of rule due to defeat in a great world war. The other has recently been defeated at the level of central executive governance by the people over whom it had ruled, also for a half century. No government simultaneously wielded authority over Taiwan and all of mainland China during the twentieth century. No government that concomitantly controlled mainland China and the island of Taiwan can claim any credit for the achievements of the Taiwanese people in the areas of capitalist economic and democratic political development in that extraordinary century. These accomplishments have come through the initiative, the tenacity, the courage, the vision, and ultimately the will of the Taiwanese people. The legacy from which these remarkable people draw as they forge an identity for the twenty-first century is only partly derived from the cultural traditions brought by immigrants from mainland China. As suggested in the exhibit at the Taibei Fine Arts Museum, the historical legacy of the Taiwanese people is at least as much composed of aborigine tradition, the colonial experience under the Japanese, and the particular adaptations in contemporary Taiwan to influences sweeping in from the Western industrial powers, most especially the United States.

Declaration of national independence by the people of Taiwan will not require that they throw off the yoke of colonial authority, as did the people who established the United States in the events after 1776. The people of Taiwan have in one manner or another already achieved independence from outsiders who imposed their rule in the twentieth century. Only mainland Chinese arrogance or international abdication of respect for the will of the Taiwanese people would result in the imposition of alien rule once more, after a declaration of independence by people who have earned the right to identify themselves as a nation before the court of international opinion. Taiwan will be an independent nation if the island's people decide that it should be. Once that decision is made, the status of nationhood could be taken away from the Taiwanese people only through the force of arms, under the watchful eye of an international community that chooses to side with contemporary might over historical right.

NOTES

1. For an excellent summary of the results of the December 1, 2001, Legislative Yuan and local elections on Taiwan, see Virginia Sheng's article, "The Voters Speak," in the monthly magazine *Taipei Review* (February 2002). Significantly, this government-funded publication had long borne the title *Free China Review,* but was given the more Taiwan-grounded appellation by the new Chen Shuibian administration immediately after the new president assumed office in 2000.

2. Chang Chiung-fang, "A Brush with Immortality: The Long and Twisted Tale of Chinese Calligraphy," *Sinorama,* August 1996, p. 33. Also see discussion of Lien Te-sen's calligraphy in Gary Marvin Davison and Barbara E. Reed, *Culture and Customs of Taiwan* (Westport, Conn.: Greenwood Press, 1998), pp. 95–96.

3. Davison and Reed, pp. 111–12; Ah Sheng, "The White Jade Ox," trans. May Li-ming Tang, *Free China Review,* March 1995, pp. 58–61, reprinted from *The Chinese PEN,* autumn 1994.

4. Davison and Reed, p. 99; Winnie Chang, "The Colors of Taiwan," *Free China Review,* October 1995, pp. 64–73.

5. Davison and Reed, pp. 106–7; Li P'eng, "The Rise of the Well-Versed Society: The Poetry Renaissance in Contemporary Taiwan," trans. Vincent Chang, *Sinorama,* December 1995, p. 129.

6. Davison and Reed, pp. 113–18.

7. Personal visits, summer 1998. The cultural sensitivity, monetary investment, and high quality of these two cultural venues that came into being during the 1990s say a great deal about the increasing sophistication of a Taiwanese society searching productively for its own identity in the twenty-first century.

8. Davison and Reed, p. 100.

INDEX

Education *(continued)*
university attendance by Taiwanese people during Japanese tenure, 65
Elections: April 1991, for National Assembly, 106; December 1995, for Legislative Yuan, 112; December 2001, for Legislative Yuan, 112; December 1991, for National Assembly, 107; December 1989, for Seats in Legislative Yuan and National Assembly, 105; Democratic Progressive Party performance in, 105; early Guomindang tenure, county and local, 77; March 1996, presidential (1991), 106; victory of Democratic Progressive Party in presidential election, March 2000, 114
Emergency Committee of the Legislative Yuan, 83
Export-led economic growth, 92
Exports, from Taiwan: during Dutch tenure, 100–11; during Guomindang tenure, 93, 104; during Qing dynasty tenure, 37–40; during Japanese tenure, 61–62

Family, Taiwanese: increasing prosperity as religious imperative of, 93
Fangsheng ("releasing life"), 27. *See also* Taiwan strait
Farmers movement, 109
Fauna, 3
February 28th Incident: background conditions leading to, 79; Chen Yi response to, 79; "clearing villages" (*qing xiang*) campaign in aftermath of, 80; description of, 79–80; February 28th Incident Settlement Committee created in response to, 79; leading to enunciation of Temporary Provisions Effective during

the Period of Mobilization for Suppression of the Communist Rebellion, 81; official government report (February 28th Incident Report) on, 107; Provincial Commission created in aftermath of, 81; summary, 124; Taibei City Council response to, 79
Feminist movement, 102, 109
Fengshan (county of Taiwan under Qing), 25, 29; in Lin Shuang Rebellion, 34
"Five cravings," 78
Flora (of Taiwan), 3
Food-processing industry: during Japanese tenure, 63
Foreign policy, during Guomindang rule of Taiwan, 97; toward Japan, 97; toward United States, 97
Formosan Youth (*Taiwan seinen*), 66
Fort Provintia (Chikan): capture by Zheng Chenggong (Koxinga), 17; founding by Dutch, 11; Guo Huaiyi attack on, 12
Fort Zeelandia (Anping), 5; capture by Zheng Chenggong (Koxinga), 17; founding by Dutch, 11
Four-year economic plans: for 1953–1956, 90; for 1957–1960, 91; for 1961–1964, 93
Fujian: province including Taiwan under Qing, 24
Fujianese: relationship with Hakka, 28

Gaoxiong (Kaohsiung), comparative forms of romanization of, xv; as area encompassed by Fengshan *xian* in early Qing, 29
Gaoxiong Incident, 101
Geography (of Taiwan), 3
Goto Shimpei, 54, 58
Governor, title and power of under Qing dynasty, 24

Japanese Aluminum Company, 70
Japanese colonial administration
(during tenure on Taiwan): banking
and credit policies of, 70; education policies of, 64–65; industrial policy on Taiwan during
World War II, 70–71; land surveys
and policies of, 54; local government, organization of, 56; militia,
organization of on Taiwan, 55;
modernization of economy and
infrastructure by, 59–63; self-rule
movement during, 56; summary of,
122; surrender in World War II by,
75; Taiwanese Literary movement
during, 66–72
Japanese nationals: land and enterprise ownership on Taiwan by,
57–58
Japanization (*ribenhua*), 77
Jianan (plain of western Taiwan), 28
Jiang Weishui, 66
Jieshou ("plunder") vs. jieshou
("receive"), 78
Jilong (Keelung), comparative forms
of romanization of, xv
Jinmen (Quemoy), 84
Joint Commission on Rural Reconstruction, 89
Junius, Robert, 10

Kangxi, comparative forms of roman-
ization, xvi; annexation of Taiwan
during reign of, 24
Ketou ("leaders of the guests"), 27.
See also Taiwan strait
Kissinger, Henry, 96
Kodama Gentaro, 54, 58
Kogakko ("common schools"), 64
Korean War, 83
Koxinga, 16. *See also* Zheng Cheng-
gong
Kuo, Shirley, 104

Labor force on Taiwan during Guomindang rule: characteristics of, 93
Lai Ho (Taiwanese author,
1894–1943), 67, 68
Lan Dingyuan: procolonization
(immigration) argument of, during
Qing dynasty, 29
Lan Tingzhen, 33
Land classification and taxation policies: Japanese colonial administration policies regarding, 54; Qing
dynasty administration policies
regarding, 35–38
Land reform, under Guomindang,
87–88: land-to-the-tiller phase, 88;
rent reduction phase, 87; results,
88; sale of public lands phase, 87
Law Sixty-Three (63), 54
Law Three (3), 55
League for the Establishment of a
Taiwanese Parliament, 66
Lee Teng-hui: as leader of Taiwan
Solidarity Union, 126; personal and
professional background of, 104;
reform agenda of, 105; summary of
importance of tenure as president,
124; as winner of first popular
election for president (1996), xii,
112
Legislative Yuan, 84
Li Chunqing, 78
Li Guoding (K. T. Li), 90
Li Wanzhu, 78, 82
Liao Wenyi (Thomas Liao), 82
Lien Chan, 113
Lin Shuangwen: death, 35; personal
background of, 34
Lin Shuangwen Rebellion, 34–35,
122. *See also* Rebellion
Lin Xiantang, 78, 82
Lin Yanggang, 112
Lin Zhengjie, 102
Literary Taiwan, 72

142   INDEX

About the Author

GARY MARVIN DAVISON is a teacher-researcher for the Academic Education Division of the Minneapolis Urban League. He is author (with Barbara E. Reed) of *Culture and Customs of Taiwan* (Greenwood, 1998).